D0607607

THE ULTIMATE
PORTFOLIO

THE ULTIMATE
PORTFOLIO

Martha Metzdorf

Cincinnati, Ohio

95 94 93 92 91   5 4 3 2 1

Library of Congress Cataloging in Publication Data

Metzdorf, Martha,
   The ultimate portfolio / Martha Metzdorf. -- 1st ed.
      p.   cm.
   Includes index.
   ISBN 0-89134-370-9
   1. Commercial art--United States--Marketing. 2. Art portfolios-
-United States.   I. Title.
   NC1001.6.M48 1990
   741.6'068'8--dc20   90-7986
                                                         CIP

Concept and Editorial Development by Diana Martin
Designed by Jay Anning

Page 143 constitutes an extension of this copyright page.

To Lyle

ACKNOWLEDGMENTS
To those who pushed, those who pulled, and those who got out of the way.
Special thanks to Fran and Lona, Jay, his nameless friend, and Diana.
Thanks to all the designers and illustrators who spared their time and materials.
Without exception, you are a generous and talented lot.

CONTENTS

INTRODUCTION

This is a book you can look forward to not needing. When you are a world-famous designer or illustrator and everyone knows what you do and has at least one beautiful coffee-table book of your work in their library, then you probably won't have to worry about putting together a portfolio. At that point, should a potential client (who has obviously lived on Mars for the last decade) request a sampling of your work, a few pieces thrown together will be powerful enough to bring in not only work from desired clients but also the plaudits of your peers. But if your work is anything short of that, this is a book you should read.

Throughout your career, your work will go through an infinite number of changes. Your portfolio reflects these changes. Where you are now is not where you were five years ago and hopefully not where you will be five years from now. By seeing how other professionals from around the country have worked out their portfolios at various stages of their careers, you may find just the idea or series of techniques to enhance your own book and make it work for you right now.

Every designer and illustrator included in this book started out showing a portfolio. Some of the work you will see is from people who don't often show portfolios anymore. But they do have to edit their work for shows, speeches, and client presentations. Each time you show your work, whether to a prospective client, your friend at the next desk, or from a podium to a large audience, you put together a portfolio of sorts. And you will continue to do so for your entire career.

Essentially, your book is not only a reflection of the best work you've done, it is also your calling card for the kind of work you want to do. By carefully directing your portfolio to the right people and presenting them with the right examples, you will get paid for executing your personal best.

That's the theory anyway. Between theory and practice is reality, a road paved with portfolios edited for the wrong audience, poorly organized, or possibly never even opened. The result is not getting work, but worse, it is not understanding why you aren't getting work and doubting your own creative abilities.

Before you ever get to the presentation stage, we'll discuss the process of studying your work, deciding what you are doing wrong and right, and showing how you can improve the right and eliminate the wrong. Then you'll see how you can best package and present what you've chosen. Most importantly, we'll help you find the answer to two very important questions: What do you want your portfolio to sell, and who do you want to sell it to?

The organization and presentation of your portfolio is but one element in your overall marketing effort. You'll also learn how to maintain continuity between your portfolio and the rest of your marketing efforts: your leave-behinds, mailers, ads, and listings in show catalogs. Whatever you use to increase your visibility should be part of an overall plan, not a series of random efforts.

If you are good enough, work hard, and have a bit of luck, you will succeed. Then you can give this book to someone else who really needs it.

This identity program was developed by Chermayeff & Geismar Associates of New York for Crane Business Paper. This photograph showing a number of applications within the program might be included in the design firm's portfolio.

HOW TO GET STARTED

No doubt about it—it's hard to sit down one afternoon and decide exactly what to do with the rest of your life. It's equally tough to look at your own creative work and decide what to keep in your portfolio and what to file. What looked great six months ago suddenly appears amateurish; you remember the trouble you had with one sample and decide there's no way you want to pursue that kind of assignment. The first step toward knowing what to include in your portfolio depends on knowing who your ideal client will be and finding that special person.

Your goal is to look at your existing work, decide exactly what markets you want to appeal to, and build the best portfolio possible to get yourself work in those markets. This section will tell you how to achieve your goal.

Precisely identifying your markets is the real key to setting out in the right direction. Don't get stalled because you can't decide on a ten-year plan. Start out by deciding what you want your markets to be for the next twelve months. Every bit of information you uncover about your potential markets will help you get on a definite road toward your goal. If you don't care about your career having a direction, then you don't need to organize yourself. But if you want to get somewhere, you must know where you're going.

Start by making a job possibilities list in general categories and then develop specific names working in those categories. As a designer, you might start by picking out packaging for the food industry; an illustrator might choose some specific publications for editorial. Then look through the myriad design industry awards annuals and pick out work you like, done by companies you'd like to work for; make a list of both the creatives involved and the clients. You might want to create a number of lists in slightly different areas.

Compare the two lists and see where they overlap. This should give you an indication of where you might start your search. Since this is a wish list in a sense, why not go for the moon? Make a short list of work you would do free, just for the opportunity to work with a specific person or for a specific firm, and include that in your mix.

Now you have a place to start. This will tell you what you want to do and where it can be done. Now you must decide if the work you have to show is compatible with the jobs for which you want to be hired. If not, you have to build a new portfolio and tailor it accordingly.

FOR THE DESIGNER

As a designer, you have the options of joining a design firm or working independently by seeking freelance work. A lot depends on your geographical location and whether or not you want to relocate. Depending on the business community in your area, you may be able to work your way into a local corporation. Chances are the corporation will have a design firm or advertising agency already in place. You can find out by calling the marketing department of the corporation.

The job possibilities for working with large corporations are broad. They include everything from a simple letterhead and business card design to a complete corporate identification program with all its applications. All forms of collateral may be developed. Examples include such diverse print work as capabilities brochures, sales and media kits, catalogs, hang tags, shopping bags, investor information, as well as in-house work such as insurance and benefits information, employee publications, and much of the business-to-business information.

Other segments of the design market to investigate include packaging and product design, promotions, or work received from an advertising agency. You may also develop a relationship with a magazine or book publisher for design work.

You will find that many architectural firms work closely with graphic designers to develop graphic systems to be used within their projects. Exhibits, signage, maps, and locations systems are also opportunities for you to explore.

For the Illustrator

As an illustrator, your markets will include advertising agencies, design groups, editorial, book jacket and interior book illustration work from publishers, direct corporate work, and specialty areas such as record album covers, movies, and other entertainment fields.

An illustrator with an established reputation can work from almost any geographical location. But if no one has ever heard of you, you have a problem. Your first priority is to establish which is most important to you at this point in your life: where you live or what work you do. If you want to live in a big city with lots of job options, fine. But obviously you can't live in an isolated, idyllic hamlet if you need to have day-to-day contact with a major corporate client. The quality of your life, how much money you require to maintain that quality, and how much you are willing to compromise for how long are all elements you must consider.

There is no use trying to put together a portfolio until you've really answered these questions. Your portfolio is only the clay waiting to be molded. It won't become anything by itself—you must shape it toward your goals. And if you don't force it to take shape, it will remain just a lump.

These decisions may not be the easiest you've had to make, but they are essential questions to be answered right here at the beginning. Once you know what market you are seeking, it becomes easier to know what kind of portfolio to build.

Speaking from Experience:
Jack Unruh
Illustrator, Dallas, Texas

When I first began to develop my portfolio, I spent a lot of nights drawing, about six months' worth. I was looking for a direction as well as experimenting with mediums. I went through a variety of instruments, inking toothpicks or popsicle sticks. I stayed with the popsicle sticks for a time, working with washes as well. Then I started using Rapidograph pens. One day I picked up a brush while I was working on an illustration and worked with both a pen and a brush. In a couple of hours, the whole drawing came together and that's when I started using ink and brush together.

Then I decided to develop my portfolio with a specific objective in mind. Bell Helicopter was a big client here in Dallas and all their work was being done by another illustrator. I researched photographs of their helicopters and did a series of illustrations and took them to the agency handling the account.

First of all, it impressed the agency that I had gone to so much trouble to do the drawings and convinced them that I would really work hard. Second, it showed them how good my work was and third, it gave me a foot in the door at the agency. They didn't use me immediately, but in a month or so they called and gave me a chance—and that was all I needed.

Where are Designers and Illustrators Flocking?

These figures were compiled by American Business Information, a company that tracks such trends through the national yellow pages listing. According to the 1989 figures, listings for graphic designers increased 10.1 percent in that year, while commercial artists listings decreased by 2.4 percent.

Graphic Designers and Design Services		Illustrators	
California	3,970	California	1,235
New York	1,264	New York	933
Texas	696	Illinois	801
Massachusetts	588	Florida	476
Washington	499	Texas	446
Florida	486	Ohio	423
Connecticut	429	Pennsylvania	352
Ohio	412	Michigan	323
Colorado	368	Wisconsin	253
Pennsylvania	326	Minnesota	234

WHERE WILL YOU FIND WORK?

The Bureau of Labor Statistics conducts an Occupational Employment Survey reflecting current employment figures and suggests future trends in particular professions. In the category that includes graphic designers and illustrators, the prospects are good. The total employment numbers for 1988 was 215,733. By the year 2000, the BLS projects a 27 percent growth rate in this area, almost double the national average growth rate in other fields. Of the total figure, 83,733 represent salaried workers, while 131,000 are self-employed. Sixty percent of the growth rate will occur in the self-employed sector.

WHY?

According to the Securities and Exchange Commission, 18,019 corporations produced annual reports in the United States in 1989.

The Newspaper Advertising Bureau states that advertising expenditures for 1989 in the United States are expected to exceed $125 billion. Daily newspapers continue to lead all other U.S. advertising media, making up 26.3 percent of total advertising expenditures. Television ranked second with 22 percent, and direct mail placed third with 17.9 percent.

Collateral work is the printed bridge that designers build for their clients, so that they may effectively reach consumers.

More dollars were spent on advertising automobiles and automotive accessories in 1989 than on any other product or service: $882,999,850. Toiletries and cosmetics come in second at $650,710,759 in expenditures, while business and consumer services follow third with $529,335,303 spent.

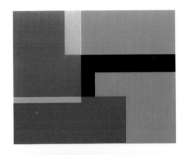

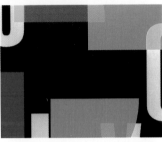

Book jacket illustration and editorial illustration for magazines constitute a major market for artists from around the world. While many publishing companies are centered in New York City, there are also a great number of regional publishers and publishers of world-wide reputation located across the country.

Corporate identity programs reflect the heart of a business. Applications are designed to be a visual shorthand reinforcing the logo. A design firm may be asked to design anything from a simple letterhead program to a complete standards manual covering all aspects of that corporation's logo and its proper usage.

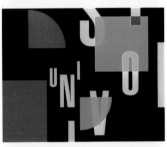

Many packaging and product design assignments are handled by in-house corporate teams, but such projects are an opportunity for both the designer and the illustrator to participate at this level of marketing.

How to Select Your Own Best Work

Now that you've got a clearer sense of the markets available, let's take a look at how to go about tailoring your portfolio to those markets by choosing the right work to include.

In assembling your portfolio, your personal likes and dislikes will have a big influence on your work over the long haul. If you hate working in a particular medium or on certain types of projects, don't include any of that kind of work in your portfolio. You must develop a showcase of work that is not only beautiful but brings you joy. Why would you pursue a segment of the profession that made you frustrated or unhappy at the outset? You'll have plenty of frustrations in jobs you like without becoming involved in jobs you don't want to do. Don't let your portfolio invite them.

You must judge your work on several levels. Try to put yourself in the shoes of your potential interviewer. What is he or she looking for? How can you make your portfolio stand out among the crowd of work he or she will be seeing? How can you specifically tailor your work and your portfolio to get the jobs you really want?

The quality, style, suitability to market, evidence of problem-solving abilities, creativity, versatility, and ability to work within a budget are all factors in deciding who gets the job. Do you have work that addresses these points? If not, then you must give yourself assignments to fill the gaps. Don't be fooled by the complexity of a piece or the story behind it. Just because you know the difficulty involved in putting something together does not mean it deserves to be in your portfolio.

Evaluating your own work is a very personal exercise. Lay out all your prospective portfolio pieces on one surface and really look at them. Is the collection visually impressive? Is the quality and production level consistent throughout? Note the deficient areas as well as the categories in which you seem to have an abundance of examples. Is this your strongest area, and are you giving this kind of work more emphasis by plan or by accident? Remember that the work you show will determine to a large extent the kind of assignments you will get, so don't put work into your portfolio you aren't prepared to deliver.

Where Do You Want to Live?

Depending on your market and your location, you may have to develop a much more horizontal approach to your portfolio. If you locate in a small market, your work will come from a broader selection of clients because there won't be enough business available from any one segment. You will have to put together a portfolio or multiple portfolios to appeal to those various segments of your market. You can't afford to specialize and you'll have to please a lot of people

If you decide to work in a major metropolitan area, you must focus your portfolio more narrowly. However, be prepared for the long haul. Don't go to New York or Los Angeles and give yourself six months to crack the market. It will take you that long to get a phone installed. Your minimum commitment should be two to three years—and this is if your work is well received and you have good luck. Three to five years is a more realistic time span in which you can expect to get your start.

How Much Money Do You Have to Make?

There is much more disparity in the pay scale for illustrators than designers, depending on the kind of work you seek. Editorial and publishing traditionally pay less than advertising. That's the bad news. The good news is that generally you are given more creative freedom. However, your questions remain the same as a designer's: you must decide who you want to work with and how important money is to you.

Now that you've answered these questions and decided exactly which markets you want to conquer, deciding what is good enough to keep and what is not in terms of your portfolio is an easier task. Not simple, just easier.

ONE ILLUSTRATION STYLE VERSUS SEVERAL

It takes an educated eye to look at a designer's portfolio and determine if he or she actually has a variety of design styles rather than a variety of projects. The nature of design jobs varies so greatly, from a logo to an annual report, that individual styles are hard to discern. Still, many designers become associated with a certain design signature. A favorite grid, a particular way of handling type—these elements become visible upon close examination. As you will see on pages 21 through 27, Kit Hinrichs' portfolios show how over the years his style has taken form and has become more refined and more sophisticated. But precisely because there is such a variety of assignments available to designers, the portfolios they show have less to do with their personal design style than with the excellence of their work in a range of different applications.

The illustrator's portfolio, however, seems to be bound by a completely different set of rules. For a long time the general wisdom was that only one style was allowed to each portfolio. But exceptions to the rule prevail. Some illustrators work in a variety of styles and they show at least some of that variety in the same portfolio.

Much depends on the size of your market. The larger the market, the more specific the portfolio. In contrast, the smaller the market, the more variety you may successfully show.

It's typical of art directors and art buyers in large cities to pigeonhole an illustrator according to one style. Frequently an illustrator will work in one style that is recognizable, and that will be the meat and potatoes of his or her work. The other styles he or she uses may work in different markets or with an art director who's aware of the versatility of the illustrator. It's easier to market just one style at a time, but that doesn't mean it has to be your only style or medium.

If you work in a variety of styles, your established clients will probably become aware of your versatility. Even so, it is confusing for an art director to see four completely different styles in one book. When an art director calls in your book, he or she probably has a job with a specific look in mind. Show your portfolio with the style that prompted the call and leave the others to be developed either through promotional pieces or a personal visit at another time.

It is up to the individual illustrator to decide what style or styles to develop and when and if to change to another. Some illustrators seem to need constant change to keep a freshness in their work or to keep from getting bored. Others are intent on the continuing refinement of what they feel is their strongest suit.

According to world-famous designer and illustrator Milton Glaser, "Inevitably you have a style if you practice long enough. You make preferences. Your eye, your mind, and your hand operate in a certain way. I think all my work is identifiable; I think it looks as though I did it, but not because I necessarily sought a particular style. I do have a style, but it isn't the style I wanted to pursue. What I really wanted to pursue was how to express ideas, how to motivate people. That is really my primary interest. The style of what I do comes out of the idea that drives it. And I've also been curious to work in a variety of mediums."

Glaser continues, "By developing an identifiable style, you have an acknowledged product to sell, one that people come specifically to you for. In the history of the United States, how people became successful was by capturing a market. People get known for specialties, for doing something that no one else does as well. The difficulty with that is, once that product has become acknowledged, it is then copied. The field is rampant with plagiarism and imitation. The person who has invested their life in this particular way of working no longer has a unique product. So this is a double-edged sword. On one hand, developing a style is a way to achieve a certain body of work and acceptance. On the other, you have to be much more resourceful if you are to have a long career in this profession."

Whichever route you choose to pursue as an illustrator, be sure that you have enough depth in your portfolio to support each of your styles. You must be able to put together a complete portfolio every time it goes out. Sacrifices are for baseball players, not portfolios.

As you can see from this selection of John Alcorn's work, a distinctive, singular style can be used in many different applications. John's work, which has won awards since the early days at The Pushpin Studio, has been incorporated in every conceivable forum, from magazine and newspaper work in Italy to packaging and book jackets.

(Above) Illustration for a poster advertising a mystery series on public television. (Top right) Cover illustration for the Italian science magazine, *Prometeo*. (Right) Illustration for packaging for Mamy Nova Yogurt. Each figure is made up of three stacking containers.

(Above, left) Illustration for the cover of *The Lamp*, Exxon's employee magazine. (Above) Jacket illustration for the book *Naso Bugiardo,* published by Rizzoli Editore Milano.

John Robinette works in a number of styles, and his portfolios are arranged accordingly. Of this arrangement, Philip Williams, his agent in Atlanta, says, "We feel John's work applies to certain kinds of assignments, and we seek them out. When we edit the book for a general call, we usually put the painterly style up front, then the acrylic work, and those are usually the only two styles we show at one time. But if we're working with someone who has used a variety of John's work, we may show his spectrum because it has so many applications as we've done here. We have editorial clients who have used all of John's styles and mediums." The examples shown on these pages range from his angular, post-modern work, to realistic and caricaturistic portraiture, to more stylized, painterly illustration.

(Above) An example of John's black-and-white pencil style, used by CIBA-GEIGY for advertising. (Above, right) Illustration for an album cover in one of John's painterly styles. (Right) John's caricature style is shown on the cover of *Memphis* magazine.

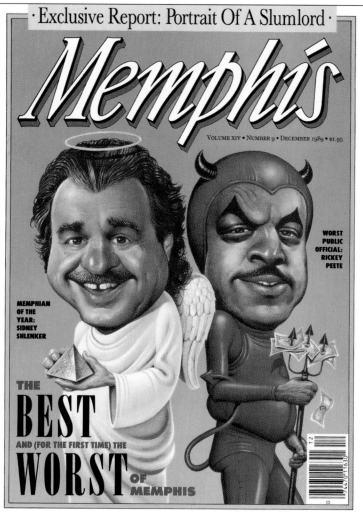

(Above, left) A personal work in oil shows John's capabilities as a fine artist. (Above) An acrylic portrait of football coach Bear Bryant in a realistic manner. (Left) An award-winning poster for a music festival features a stylistic portrait of Mark Twain and his fictional characters.

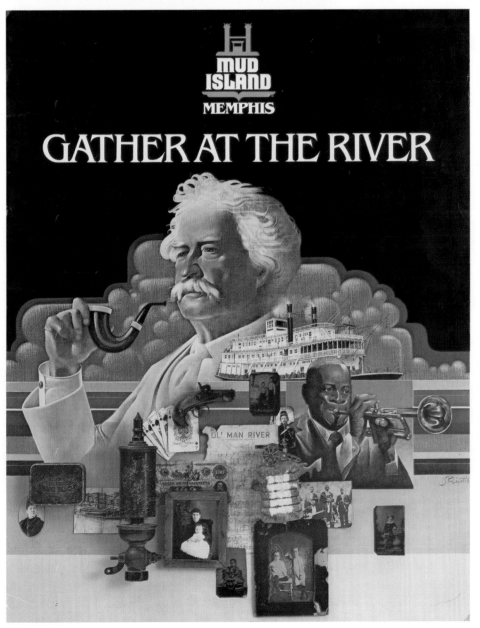

THE EVOLUTION OF A PORTFOLIO

Kit Hinrichs, a principal of Pentagram Design, grew up in California. One Saturday morning while still in high school, he was cleaning out a garage and ran across an old government pamphlet that announced, "You can earn $15 to $25 apiece for commercial illustrations." Eureka! Kit had found his calling, and he immediately approached his art teacher to ask for confirmation of this wondrous opportunity. At the teacher's suggestion, he put together his first portfolio for submission to Art Center College of Design in Pasadena. The year was 1959.

Kit still works at his portfolios, although today they are quite different in scope and refinement. The evolution of his portfolio reflects the evolution of his skills and career directions and the variety of his clients. From his early days in school to the sophisticated presentations available to him today, it is reassuring to watch simple but solid beginnings develop into some of the most memorable and informative design work in the world.

Kit's high school graduation portfolio consisted of an African mask created with cut paper, a Halloween poster in tempera on poster card (which he considered a design piece as well as illustration since he did all the lettering), and about ten other school projects, most of which were illustration pieces. He uniformly mounted each piece on black board, put them in his case, and submitted it to the review committee. His work was good enough to be part of the ten percent or so of students accepted to Art Center directly from high school.

Shortly after arriving at Art Center, Kit's portfolio went through drastic changes. While illustration had been the focus of his early work, now advertising was added to the mix. An assignment in his first advertising class was accomplished with the help of his dad. The visual was a kangaroo with boxing gloves, his pouches filled with oranges, leaning against orange crates. The copy line read, "No matter how you box them, California oranges are your best punch for lunch." Kit says of this today, "My teacher was speechless."

Kit graduated in 1963 with a degree in advertising design and headed directly to New York City with every intention of becoming an art director at an advertising agency. His book showed advertising and illustration even though Kit excelled at collateral, and about half the portfolio was corporate-oriented projects. Although he had not considered interviewing with a design firm, after he showed his portfolio he landed a job as a junior designer.

Most of his school portfolio was discarded because half of it was devoted to advertising. Kit sought collateral design work and developed a reputation as a freelance editorial illustrator. His portfolio again changed. In the late 1960s Kit had the opportunity to design and install exhibits. The design and illustration work was shown in sample form in his portfolio. The exhibit work was recorded on 35mm slides.

"In the early days [when I was partnered] with Tony Russell [now principal of Anthony Russell, Inc., in New York City]," Kit remembers, "we made up a portfolio of what we had done. Since we hadn't done a lot, we didn't have a lot to show, so we had to arrange it well and make sure it was always perfect. Often we took the same pieces out each time we showed our work because it was not only the best, but the only thing we had. We had both advertising and illustration in our portfolio, and our primary market was editorial sources and advertising agencies."

Now, as a Pentagram partner in San Francisco, Kit's work is shown with that of the rest of the partners' in portfolio presentations to clients. "We can show not only the work that comes out of our office, but the offices in New York and London as well. We have such resources and depth on our staffs, and we want to be sure our portfolios reflect that capability," Kit says.

"When we make up a portfolio at Pentagram, we tend to make it up to reflect the client's business. If, for instance, the client is in the travel business, we will show a range of work we've done related to the travel industry rather than a range of collateral pieces from different businesses. We feel that in this way the client has the chance to see the scope of work we can provide for him as well as our level of excellence.

"Our presentations depend entirely on the nature of the meeting, and that is determined by as many phone calls as it takes for us to determine what the client problems are. Keeping the problem in mind will help you determine what to include in your portfolio.

"For an opening meeting, we might take a half dozen samples of our work in a briefcase just to let them get a feel for what we do. These samples will represent a range of our work. A meeting on a more formal level may call for a two slide-tray presentation or something more complex. We tailor the presentation to the client in every case. The format may change, depending on the number of people involved in the presentation. For a large group, you almost have to use slides, but for a presentation to one or two key executives, we tend to use as many actual samples as possible. I feel that the design business appeals to the tactile sense as well, and I want them to be able to 'feel' our good work as well as see it.

"One additional nuance to our presentations now is the informational material that is either sent ahead or left behind after the presentation. We also use 'Pentagram Papers' and our book, *Ideas On Design,* to expand on our presentation."

The surviving examples of Kit's portfolio from his Art Center days are personal illustrations of Germany and an advertisement for suntan preparation done as a student assignment.

Tan yourself with a golden glow, a reflection of the sun's own color, perfected for you by Revlon—it's name...Sun Bath

On these pages we see how
Kit's portfolio began to
develop and mature in the
early 1960s. He showed a full
mix of illustration, advertising,
and design work to his clients.
(Left) Posters for the Chase
Manhattan Bank in New York
City show the beginnings of a
design signature that will be
carefully refined in the coming
years. (Above) A calendar for
the William Sloan YMCA.

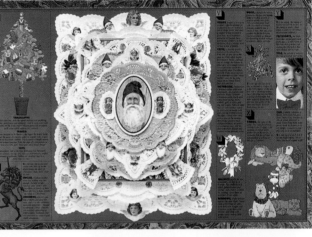

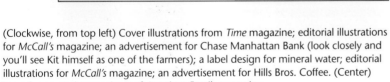
(Clockwise, from top left) Cover illustrations from *Time* magazine; editorial illustrations for *McCall's* magazine; an advertisement for Chase Manhattan Bank (look closely and you'll see Kit himself as one of the farmers); a label design for mineral water; editorial illustrations for *McCall's* magazine; an advertisement for Hills Bros. Coffee. (Center) Logo for an anniversary issue of *American Family* magazine.

In the late 1970s, Kit dropped all illustration work from his portfolio and he began to concentrate on designing. Much of his work came from the corporate arena. (Clockwise from right) Self-promotion work for Kit's first design group (exemplifying what Kit calls his "Seymour Chwast period"); the Warner Communications 1976 Annual Report, Kit's first big break in corporate design; the Warner Communications 1977 Annual Report.

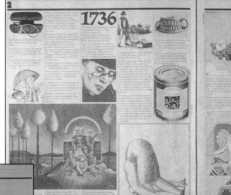

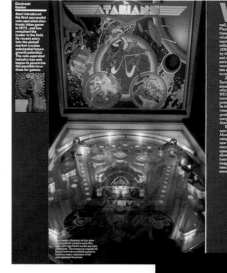

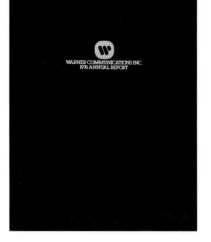

In the early 1980s, Kit's portfolio reflected a continuation and refinement of his corporate work. (Left) Sales promotion for the Oakland Athletics baseball team. (Center, left) The Potlatch Corporation 1983 Annual Report. (Center, right) The MGM/UA 1986 Annual Report. (Bottom) Poster design for the San Francisco chapter of the American Institute of Graphic Arts, which is in the poster collection of the Museum of Modern Art, New York.

This spread shows the most recent Kit Hinrichs/Pentagram San Francisco portfolio. (Right) Cover, spread, and gatefold from the Immunex 1988 Annual Report. (Below) Cover and spread from *Skald* magazine, the magazine of the Royal Viking Line.

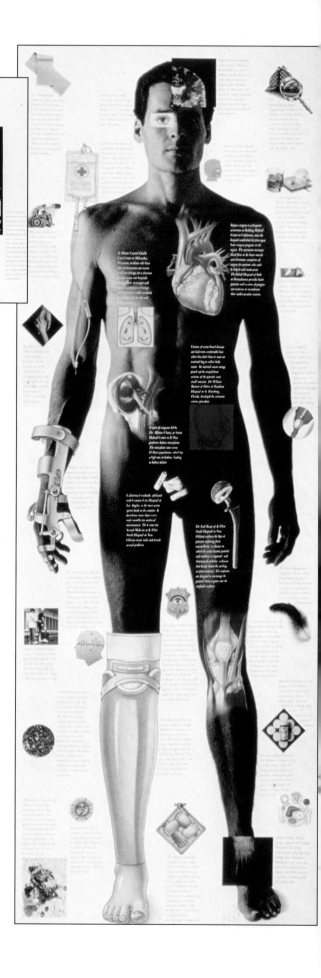

THE ULTIMATE PORTFOLIO

(Below) Calendar for the American President Companies. (Center, right) Catalog spread, cover, and product design for The Nature Company. (Bottom right) *Stars & Stripes* and *Vegetables* book jackets (Kit was responsible for the development and design of each book in its entirety).

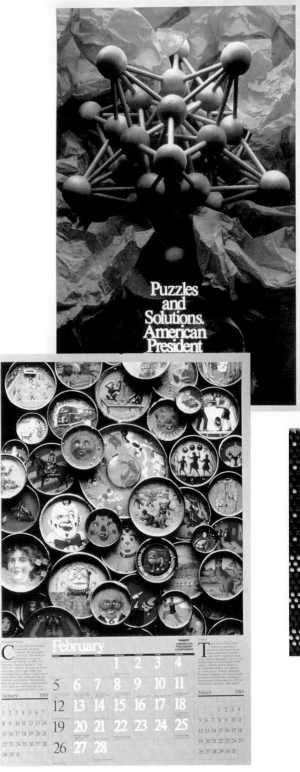

EDITING YOUR PORTFOLIO

Editing is not simply eliminating from your portfolio those pieces that do not belong, it is the art of preparing your presentation by its arrangement. The order in which you present your portfolio pieces will set the pace, the impact, and the overall mood of your work. Whether you're putting together a ten-piece illustration portfolio or a full slide tray of design projects, you have the same goal: You want the viewer to be swept away. You want whoever reviewed your portfolio to think about your images on the way home in the evening and again when they wake up in the morning. In short, you want them to be motivated to call and give you a job.

We're going to address different kinds of portfolios in this section, that is, portfolios put together for different purposes. While the editing techniques used will stay pretty much the same, the focus of the books will change considerably.

There are some known and unknown factors to deal with in editing. Sending a portfolio off in response to a potential client's request is the easiest. The known factors are the pieces to include. They'll be determined largely by the call for your portfolio. You'll know who called, whether or not they have seen your work, and if so, what kind of work they have seen and a little about the specific job they have in mind. If you are trying to solicit work from a potential client who is unfamiliar with your work and where there is no specific job, then your pieces will be determined by the research you have done on the client and the type of work they do.

If your portfolio is called in on a specific job, you'll have a rough idea of that job, and the kind of work you include will be the most relevant to the job. Breaking into a new market or introducing your work to new people calls for a different type portfolio, a general portfolio that will serve as your formal introduction.

When you make a "cold call," one in which you initiated the appointment and the person you are seeing is not familiar with your work, you will put together a more general portfolio. This general portfolio must be broader in focus than the more specific book you would produce for a specific job. You want to show the breadth and depth of your work, to show all the possibilities. You still want to edit with the strongest pieces at the opening and closing, but the pieces you include will cover assignments from a variety of clients and for a variety of jobs.

If you have just moved to a new area and are starting the process of meeting all your prospective clients, this is the book you'll use. As you develop relationships with art directors or designers, you will show them more narrowly focused work or different styles. This doesn't mean that you should dig up all the life-drawing work from school or the series of nicely done but boring graphs you did for an insurance brochure. It does mean you should show examples of all the kinds of major work you want to do. It's fine to include a few pieces of personal work, and this is probably the best time to show it.

As you present this overview, be aware that the person will be interviewing you as much as your work, especially at the outset. Always remember that you are selling yourself as well as your work through your portfolio.

THE POST & RAIL EDITING TECHNIQUE

Think of organizing your portfolio in the same way you would build a fence. Designate your very best pieces as fence posts, the strength of your fence. The number of strong pieces you have will determine how long your fence is. Think of the remainder of the pieces as the rails that join one post to the next.

First, pick out the three best pieces you have in order, first, second, and third. Open your portfolio with piece number one, close your book with piece number two, and use piece number three in the middle. The position of these three best examples will be the strong points that establish your work's quality and substance. You will connect the remaining "rail" pieces to each of these strong posts to complete the building of your fence.

The opening piece for an illustrator might be the cover of a prestigious international publication (or, if you're just starting out, any piece that has been published or used by a client). A designer might begin with an award-winning project. It's best to open with something that subliminally shows approval. It's a vote of confidence about your work and gives the rest of your work the same sense of validation. This piece will set the tone of your portfolio. It represents the style you want to be remembered by and positions your work in the art director's mind.

While it's absolutely mandatory to open with a smashing work, it's equally important to close with a great piece. The final impression is almost as important as the first impression. And keep in mind that if you are using a bound portfolio to show your work, many art directors first thumb through your book from back to front; this is another reason why the first and last images are the two most important. If your presentation is in slide-tray form, the final image may be the first topic of conversation after the lights come back up and the segue between your portfolio and the offer of a brand-new assignment.

If you can develop a story or a reason to pause at the middle piece, you can further control the pace at which your work is reviewed. Use the opportunity to explain this "story piece" to your advantage; tell how you solved a particularly thorny problem or offer a brief, humorous anecdote about the piece. Use this example to personalize this meeting. Form a bridge with your interviewer and your portfolio. And recalling the story will help them remember your work.

Now look at the remainder of the pieces you pulled to include in this portfolio, the pieces we designated as "rails." Think of them in terms of horizontal or vertical, black-and-white versus color, or any other physical dissimilarities. If the format of the portfolio you use allows facing pages, you must consider the juxtaposition of your works. If there is no subject theme you need to edit for, then work out what flows best with your eye. Connecting one to the next, from rail to post, is this basic editing technique.

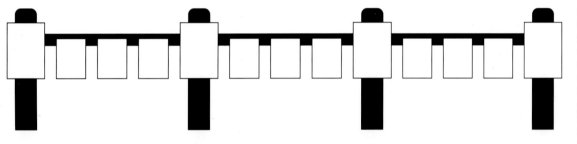

Build your portfolio the way you would a fence. Your best work will be the foundation, the "posts" that hold the portfolio together. In between will be your "rails," linking the strongest pieces together and giving an idea of the full range of your work.

SPECIAL EDITING TECHNIQUES FOR DESIGNERS

In order to develop a design portfolio, which may include a wide range of work, the editing technique must change to allow for the different categories. Since you will have an idea of the type of work the prospective client wants to see, you will know which of your examples you want to show. Opening and closing with the strongest pieces, even in mini-categories, will give you the same results. Instead of picking single pieces, you may choose a series of works that represent a comprehensive design program. Deciding how many of these programs to show will obviously depend on how many you have to show and the range of work you have done.

Many designers like to show the broadest range of work they do so that the client can appreciate the entire scope of the firm. If, for example, a retail company calls on the design firm to work on hang tags for a product, the firm might show not

only other hang tags, but point-of-sale, promotions, gift boxes, and the annual report they had prepared for for a previous assignment. This would make up one section of the total portfolio. Depending on the level of this meeting (whether it is an initial meeting or one with a higher level of management), the firm may put together a series of case histories of projects created for a variety of their clients and order the histories in the same post-and-rail technique.

Normally, the work of the design firm will be presented as a whole; that is, no one partner's work separated from the others. However, there are exceptions to that rule. In the case where the work of two artists are shown in one portfolio, the two artists should decide between them whose work will be shown first and whose will close the portfolio. Any collaborative work will be the segue between the two.

DOUGLAS FRASER

THE GENERAL ILLUSTRATION PORTFOLIO

In this section you'll see the post-and-rail technique go into action. Douglas Fraser is a young illustrator who lives and works in Calgary, Canada. His illustrations have appeared in a number of different venues, from corporate annual reports to editorial features and advertising campaigns. For the following pages, Douglas will sort through a selection of his work as an example of how he develops his general illustration portfolio.

Although he is now a successful professional illustrator, the basis for Douglas's editing process began in his days at art school. Reflecting on this period, he says, "When I was a student at the School of Visual Arts in New York City, there were things going on in the background of my personal sketchbooks that I never showed in any of my portfolios because I was not clear myself as to how I felt about the work. The style that I am working in now would rise later.

"The most growth in my work has gone on within my personal sketchbooks. As a student, I was struggling to harness this new work. I needed to be able to bring it out of the shadows and into the light, and get a grip on what I wanted to do.

"Being in a classroom setting and confronted by some who were not exactly swept up with what I wanted to do forced me to defend myself. These critiques were not a picnic, but it was the process of standing up and defending myself that blew away a lot of the weaker aspects of what I was trying to resolve, and left a hardened core of what I was trying to do. My work became more directed and I grew a lot during those bouts.

"Taking your own portfolio around isn't comfortable, but it is rewarding. The experience helps you understand exactly what art directors want to see, how they see your work, and which pieces in your book works and which don't. It is a time for clarification. It is also a time when you will learn to defend your art.

"Confronting people with your portfolio elicits a wide range of responses. Some people are swept away, some sit on the other side of the table, speechless and blank-faced. You get a handshake and a 'Thank you very much. We'll call you.' The worst of all is the impersonal drop-off. If your portfolio is opened at all, you consider yourself fortunate. Sometimes there is an impersonal form letter, and if you're lucky you get a personalized statement from the person who's seen it, like 'Great Stuff' or 'Love It.'

"I was living with two other illustrators during my second year of school and we shared dirt-cheap space. We needed to sell work to help cover the costs of living in the city, so we showed our portfolios as often as possible. In the evenings, we used to sit around laughing and comparing our form letters. We eventually built such a collection, we wallpapered the kitchen with them.

"Now the work shown in my portfolio basically reflects the work I like and what I want to do. I try to pick topics I like to work with rather than identify specific jobs. I'm more concerned about subject matter and design than who I do it for. The line drawn between the art direction on advertising and editorial is a little antiquated. I have worked for some publications where the art direction was so heavy-handed that it made advertising look like a breath of fresh air. I can't say one is better than the other. I just say let's hear about what they want."

In his portfolio, Douglas prefers to show work in its original form rather than in context. "When I first started out, I wanted as many printed pieces in my book as possible. Over the last couple of years, I find that I am phasing out the printed work and just showing my illustrations. I feel they are strong enough to stand on their own. If the image works, the portfolio works. The art is served up front and center. If there is just a drop-off policy, then I like to identify how each piece was used with a caption or a group of captions listed on a separate page."

For the purposes of editing a general portfolio, Douglas will identify all fifteen pieces and then edit out five. Normally, you would be showing about twenty pieces, but this exercise will take you through the basic steps of the process.

An illustration of a Soviet worker by Douglas Fraser for the cover of *Business Week* magazine.

An illustration used as a book cover by Knopf. It's a dramatic piece and should be included, but only as a transition.

This is a strong piece and I'll use it as a post. A double-page ad, it was published widely in business magazines such as *Forbes* and *Business Week* and I want clients to see how I can illustrate an abstract idea.

This is an example of my muralesque work and while I'm called upon to do this type of thing a lot, I don't want to be known only as a muralist. I want to show this piece in the portfolio, but I don't want to emphasize it.

My strongest piece—I'll use it to open the book because I think the iconography is classic. I like to open with an editorial illustration because generally it's more personally interpretive. This was used for the cover of *Business Week*

I like this illustration because it shows a positive response to AIDS in the workplace. Because it shows a different approach to a critical problem, I want to use it in a rail position in the portfolio.

My first major public art assignment was this mural, painted 14'x46' on an Oakland freeway at the factory location. It has earned a Heritage Award from the city and is on permanent display. Again, I want to include it, but not with great emphasis.

I did this work for the Oakland A's baseball team. It's a different application of my work, done for a different audience. Therefore I'll use it as a rail piece.

This piece is good, but too similar to the woman in front of the sink. I like that one better so I'll drop this one from the book.

A lot of people are uncomfortable with this piece. It's less powerful than the Soviet worker, but I still like it. I have a real struggle whether to use this or not, but in the end, I think the Soviet piece is stronger. This is too similar to that one, so I'll have to let it go.

This is an editorial piece, done for a special issue of *Adweek* magazine. The subject was marketing and consumerism in the 1990s and it was a chance to combine pop art, distinctive coloration, and a muralist technique. This is my most recent work and represents the kind of assignments I want to get, so I'll use it as the closing piece in my portfolio.

This is too much like the other murals I've already selected, and since it's the oldest of the three, I'll eliminate it.

I want to include this calendar piece because again it appeals to a more general audience, instead of the more limited corporate environment.

I want to use this piece close to the front of the book since it refers to a timely political situation. It's not strong enough to be used as a post, but it works well as a rail, because while it's slightly different from the other pieces, it complements them.

A personal illustration, this one doesn't have as broad an audience as the baseball piece. The two are similar and I don't want them to compete. I'll eliminate this one.

This illustration is on the same general topic as the Soviet piece and that piece is better. I'm taking this one out.

THE ULTIMATE PORTFOLIO

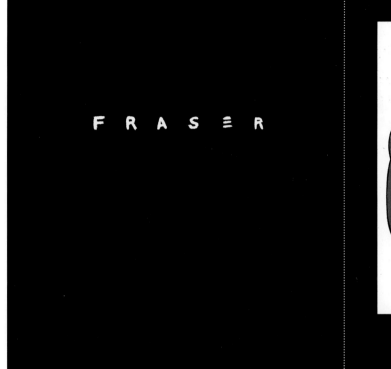

Post One: *Soviet Worker,* a cover for *Business Week* magazine.

Rail: Inside illustration for *Regardie's* magazine.

Rail: Program cover for the Oakland A's.

Rail: Page from a calendar on the topic of AIDS.

Post Two: Nationally published advertisement for Allan Bradley, a computer software manufacturer.

Rail: Book jacket for Knopf.

Rail: Page from a calendar of events for the California Performing Arts of San Francisco.

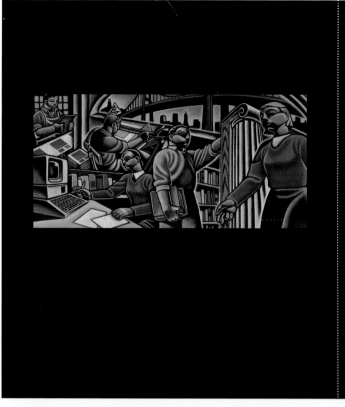

Rail: A mural for the San Francisco Summer Jobs Program.

Rail: Tasco mural, a public art installation.

Post Three: Editorial illustration for *Adweek* magazine.

THE JOB INTERVIEW PORTFOLIO

This portfolio probably gets the angst award for all time. To reduce the time you spend soul-searching, editing, and muttering to yourself, let's go back a step to what you should think of before you even get to the portfolio. If you're looking for a job with a design firm, regardless of their size or your experience, you are asking them to invite you to become a part of their family. Do you know what kind of work this firm does? Do you know the principals involved in the firm, and do you admire their work? Do you want to work for a firm this size and in this market? Is there an opportunity for growth in an area you want? Is the salary level appealing?

Regardless of their geography, designers tell me that finding good people is one of their most difficult and important tasks. Almost unanimously the first thing they say is that they are looking for smart people who are serious about their work. Yes, they want you to have a great book, but they also expect you to articulate the thinking behind your book, to be able to fit into their established group without making waves and stirring up office politics, and to be enthusiastic. Obedience and thrift were seldom mentioned. Intelligence almost always came first. The bottom line here is that hand skills don't replace brains.

Steff Geissbuhler of Chermayeff & Geismar Associates in New York City says, "We are looking for intelligence, true intelligence. Someone who can understand and communicate. When we hire someone, we expect that person to assert himself and learn as much as he can. We like self-starters. If you have a question, stop, get the answer, and go on. Know when to ask and when to act. Become a part of us. We throw junior designers in a project and expect them to take on a lot of responsibility—much more than is usually offered at other design firms. We expect a lot of our people, and if they don't want the responsibility, they won't be happy here. We try to find people who accelerate beyond the bounds of their job description very quickly. Whether as junior designers or on an internship or in production, it doesn't matter; they show that they are responsible, so you

give them something more each time. They have succeeded–they have matched our expectations."

Steff suggests that when you are preparing your portfolio, inside and out, you consider it a design problem. "It's not necessary to buy something expensive. You can make your own creative presentation. You do a cover and a title which has to work with the book and make it up just as you would have with an assignment for a client. The résumé you submit should show your deftness with type and page layout. You should make the whole presentation like a gift, something you want to open, perhaps with an element of surprise."

Claudia De Castro has just been hired by Pinkhaus Design in Miami, Florida. This is her first job after graduating from Florida State University. She is sharing her portfolio with her comments about the time and care she took to assemble it and what she chose to include.

Joel Fuller, president of Pinkhaus, who conducted the interview, said that when he saw Claudia's portfolio, he did not have an opening. After looking at her book, he thanked her, she left, and he thought about her book for the next week. He decided she showed so much potential that he had to make a place for her in his shop.

Claudia decided on an 18"x24" spiral-bound, vinyl sleeve case to hold her work, which was mounted on black boards. She wanted the larger size to give each piece enough space around it—she wanted the work to look important and not be crowded. Because of the heat and humidity in Miami, she used vinyl instead of acetate; she also felt the vinyl would be less destructive to her Chromatec pieces.

"I must have turned each page at least a hundred times to make sure they turned smoothly. I used only right-hand pages and wanted to control exactly where the viewer's eye would fall on each page. Movement and lighting were all elements I considered. It took me two months to find the right portfolio case, and then I had to special order the size I wanted.

"The only time I used both left- and right-hand pages was when I had to show a project that had several elements. It needed the space, and I laid out the page as a spread. I had everything mounted against black because I felt it made my work stand out from the page. I used no captions because this was not a drop-off situation. Besides, I wanted the opportunity to answer questions and develop a dialogue with my interviewer. I found out about Pinkhaus Design through an article in *HOW* magazine. They were the only place in the city of Miami I considered."

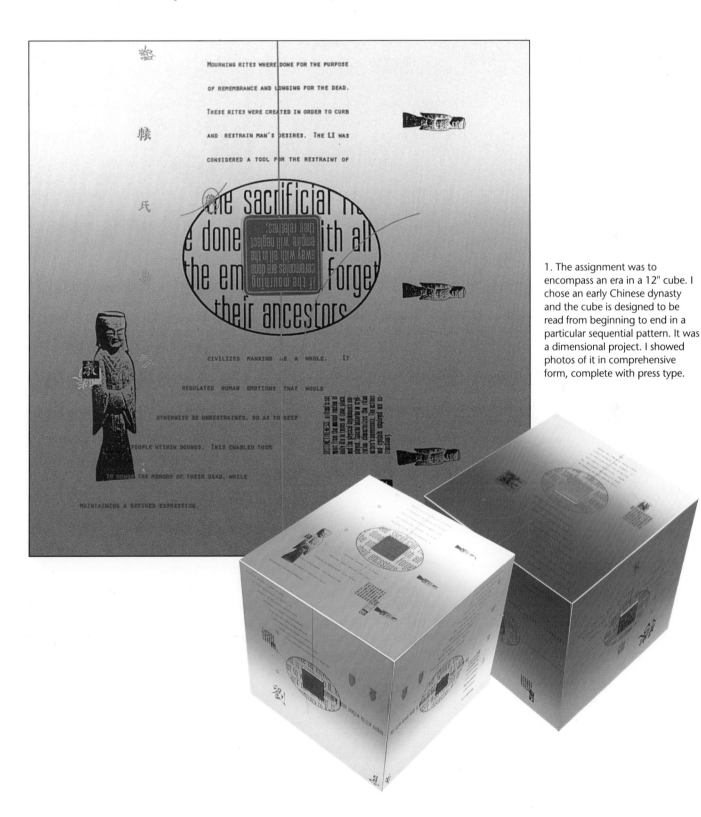

1. The assignment was to encompass an era in a 12" cube. I chose an early Chinese dynasty and the cube is designed to be read from beginning to end in a particular sequential pattern. It was a dimensional project. I showed photos of it in comprehensive form, complete with press type.

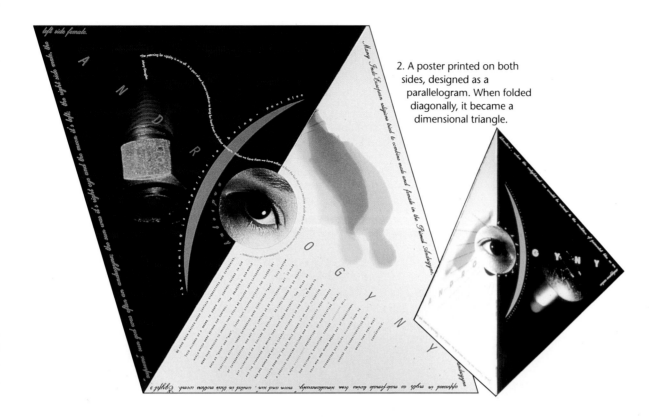

2. A poster printed on both sides, designed as a parallelogram. When folded diagonally, it became a dimensional triangle.

3. This was a blue-print assignment and I wanted to use it in my portfolio because it shows how I handle type.

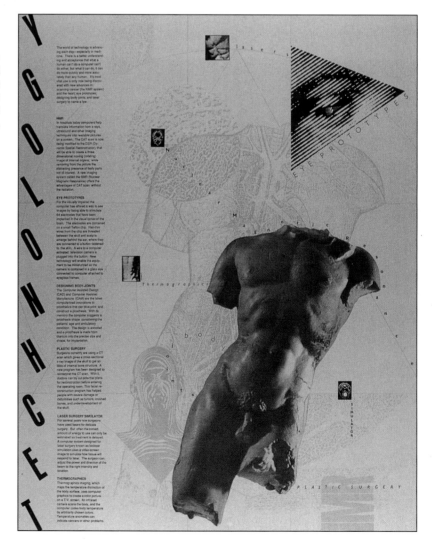

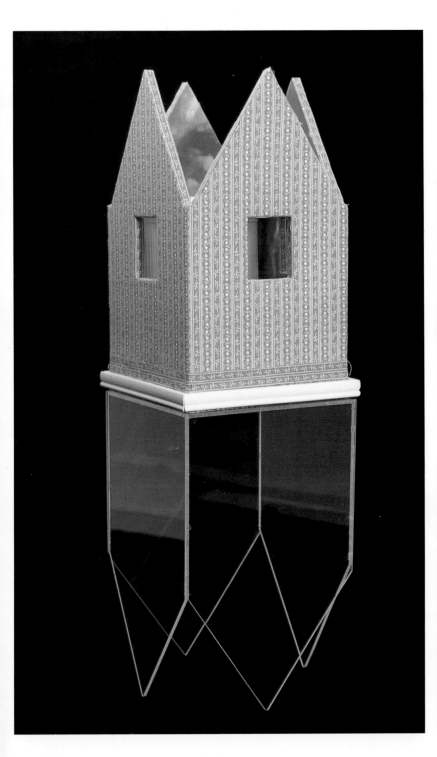

4.-6. The assignment was to package the proverb "People who live in glass houses should not throw stones." This is a dimensional project I showed in color photocopy form. I went through a lot of photocopies before I got the right color balance. It was very difficult to show all the aspects of this project, but I felt it was important to include because of its complexity.

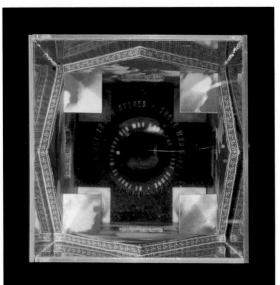

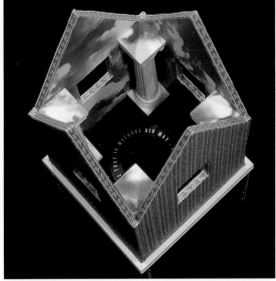

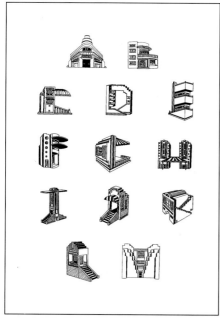

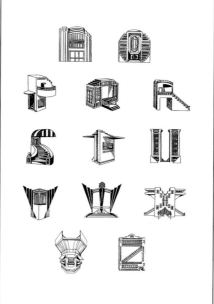

7.-8. I designed this alphabet in pen and ink. The basis for the letter forms was the art deco style of Miami architecture. I spent weekends photographing different buildings and doing library research. The result was published in *U&lc* magazine and during the interview Joel remembered seeing it. That was great because it saved my having to work it into the conversation. I made photostats of the original boards and reduced them for my portfolio. Joel later told me that this was the piece that impressed him the most.

9. When I was at school, I put up signs announcing that I would design any piece for the university for free, as long as I retained design control. In this way I developed experience working with clients and a budget, while collecting printed pieces for my portfolio. This piece was created for the music department at Florida State.

THE ULTIMATE PORTFOLIO

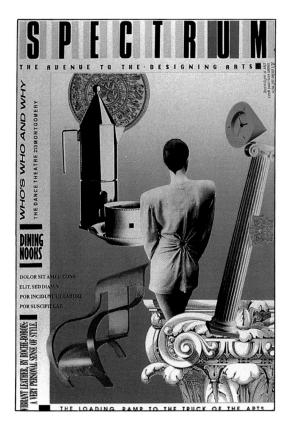

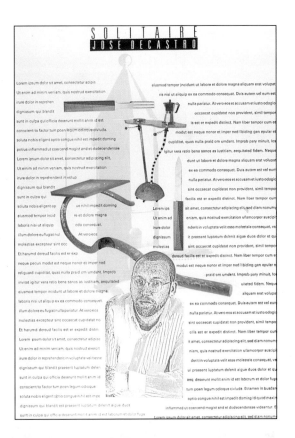

10.-12. These are magazine cover comps and an inside spread from a school project. I felt these were important to show, because the assignment included so many elements of design and I wanted to demonstrate my abilities in each area.

13.-14. This is another example of a printed poster done for the music department. It started out as a two-color job and after budget cuts ended up as black-and-white. I really had to work with money constraints on this. It was unlike most student projects, which typically have no budgetary restrictions.

15. My personal stationery, created as a student project. I designed it as a one-color job to keep the costs down and I showed the actual printed pieces in my portfolio.

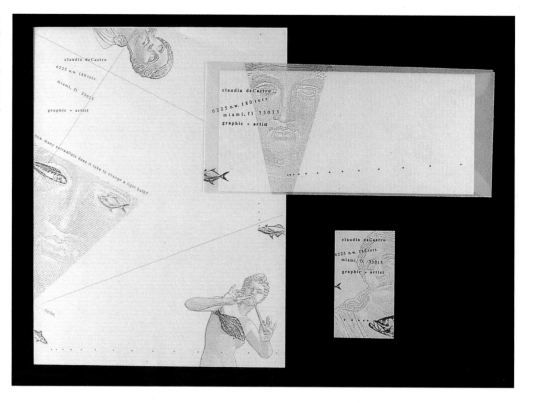

16. I closed with this piece because it is my award winner. It was designed as an entry to a yearly competition sponsored by the Capitol Engraving Company of Miami. The theme was "Color by Numbers," and my entry was created with cut paper. I won the top prize, which not only included a cash award, but also gave me a professionally printed piece for my book.

THE ILLUSTRATOR'S EDITORIAL PORTFOLIO

Editorial work is often the first foot in the door for illustrators. It offers high visibility, an opportunity to work under generally less restrictive art direction than advertising, and is one of the traditional ways to build up your portfolio with published work. The down side of editorial is the pay. Advertising can often pay four to five times the rate of editorial, depending on the complexity of the illustration and the usage. It's not just that advertising pays so much more; it's also that many magazines' illustration rates have not had to keep pace with other segments of the market. According to Paul Basista, executive director of the Graphic Artists Guild, in the 1920s and 1930s, some of the national consumer publications like the *Saturday Evening Post, Harper's,* and *Collier's* paid about $3,000 for a cover illustration. In the sixth edition of the *Pricing and Ethical Guidelines Handbook,* the rate today for national consumer publications is $3,500. Still, lots of editorial is assigned to illustrators every day, and while you may not get rich, you can pay some bills.

While it's true most of the magazine work is centered in New York City, that doesn't mean you have to be in New York to get assignments. It just means that you have to put together a portfolio directed specifically toward the editorial market.

Dave Jonason, an illustrator from Washington, D.C., is an example. Dave started out on his own, seeking assignments through a mailer that he designed and had printed. He developed a mailing list with the names of 1,000 potential clients and sent it out. The response was enough to cover the cost of the promotion, but he soon found himself bogged down in the business of negotiations, billings, seeking new clients—in short, the business of an illustrator away from the board. Dave decided to find a representative. He wanted one in New York, so he began researching and chose The Pushpin Group. Reflecting on his naiveté in the business, Dave remembers that when he signed up with Pushpin, he thought "there was soon going to be a mailbox full of checks" because

of the firm's reputation. It took about eight to nine months for work to begin rolling in on a regular basis, and this is quite normal. A good client base is slow to build and must be carefully constructed. According to Dave, "It's worked out well. The assignments have grown in size and complexity as I have learned to deal with them. If I had received some of the larger and more complicated assignments I'm doing now in the beginning, I would have been completely overwhelmed."

In order to break into the illustration market, Dave and his rep at The Pushpin Group, Nancy Schwartz, started out seeking editorial assignments. "We use tearsheets mounted on black railroad board covered with .003 acetate with black tape around the sides. Labels are affixed to the back so that each piece is identifiable, and a specific portfolio is made up for each call. We use a case that is designed to hold 8½" x 14" pieces."

On these pages Nancy will take us through a portfolio that she has edited for Dave. It includes examples of magazine covers, full inside pages, and spot illustrations.

1. This is the logical opening piece. It's powerful and eye-catching, and was published as a cover for *Frankfurter Allgemeine Magazin,* a major international magazine.

2. I follow the opener with another cover illustration (for *Math Puzzles* magazine) with wonderful color. Together, they create a one-two punch.

3. A cover illustration for *Mortgage Banking* magazine appears third. The sequence works well, and opens the book powerfully.

4. An inside editorial piece for *World Tennis* magazine. It was well executed and exhibits how well Dave's style may be used for a variety of subjects.

5. I place this strong inside piece—created for *Business Week*—in the middle because people almost always pause over this illustration, and it helps me set the pacing of the interview.

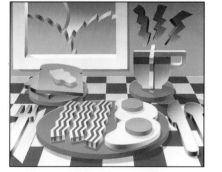

6. This was Dave's original self-promotion piece, and we used it in the portfolio from the start. In fact, we have sold usage rights several times on this work.

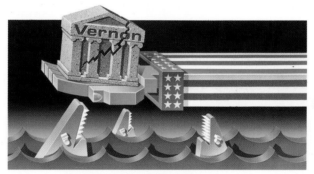

7. This large, inside spot illustration for *Money* magazine is a good sample of Dave's work for inside pages. Depending on the quality of the reproduction and the usage, we may show this kind of work in context or in its original form.

9. I like the movement in this piece done for *Mortgage Banking*, and it's a good lead-in to the closing illustration.

8. Along with the *Money* magazine sample shown above right, this completes a pair of strong inside illustrations. It was for *Outlook* magazine.

10. It's dramatic, it's a knockout, and it's a cover from the same international magazine as the opener. There's a real sense of continuity in the editing of this portfolio. It's like a completed circle.

THE ILLUSTRATOR'S DESIGN PORTFOLIO

"I really like working for good designers," says illustrator Jack Unruh of Dallas. "They have great projects, they let me use my imagination, and they pay well." Jack's work graces a range of corporate collateral assignments, including annual reports, promotional pieces, and calendars. His work also appears in advertising and publications. From ads for the *Wall Street Journal* to illustration work in *National Geographic* magazine, his drawings translate well across a broad range of topics.

When he shows his portfolio to a designer for a new assignment, Jack includes samples from all sources to help the designer better understand his range and the direction an illustration might take. "In design work there may be more creative alternatives available than in advertising work. The designer may know the feel of what he wants, but he doesn't have to have a guy with a can of dog food in his right hand and his left hand patting the head of his faithful companion. We talk about what he wants and then I try to put together the best examples from my work for the job."

Jack likes to send printed samples as a large part of his presentation to show how his work has been used. He feels showing the work in context gives the viewer an overall sense of how the illustration works with the design to form a unit. Obviously, he shows the work in this form only when the design is great. "I don't want to have to apologize for or defend anything I send out." When he has been published in a brochure that also includes the work of other illustrators, he will mark the page on which his work appears. "I don't take the book apart and just send my page. I don't mind showing my work next to that of other illustrators. I feel my work can stand on its own merits."

Since he does more than half his work out of town, Jack tries to keep all his portfolio samples in a form that can be easily boxed and sent out. Individual pieces of pure illustration and all outsized pieces are recorded on a 4"x5" or 35mm transparency format, so they may be included and easily viewed

"I think designers are more sensitive to the presentation of your illustration than are art directors at advertising agencies. Generally speaking, agency people tend to look at a lot more illustration than designers. The art buyers have files of all the creative services, and if an art director wants a quick reference, he's used to seeing what the buyer can pull out of a file at a moment's notice. At design firms you usually deal one on one with the designers right from the start of the job."

Jack tries to keep a list of the pieces he sends out and attaches it to the shipping receipt on a portfolio request. "I always request the return of my samples and try very hard to keep up. It's difficult enough to get a good supply of samples from the client, but even harder to keep them. Keeping them, storing them, and retrieving them are part of the chores of the illustration business."

1.-3. These first three portraits are from the Triton Energy Corporation Annual Report. The Bangkok woman is on the cover of the report and the Gabon portrait is an award winner in the Society of Illustrators show. I think it's a strong opening presentation.

4. This was a calendar page illustrating the monk who invented Benedictine brandy. It is a personal favorite and a good contrast to the first set of portraits.

5. I include this piece because it was the cover of the New York Art Directors Club call for entries and it's not people, animals or mythical things.

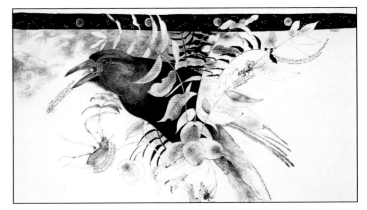

6. To show I can do something other than portraits, I like to introduce this side of my work, wildlife illustration. This was done for a Mead Paper Company book.

7. This is Henry Ford as an old man, living besieged on his father's farm, done for a Simpson Paper Company book. I like the emotion this illustration presents. It forms a real link with the viewer.

8. This portrait of Morgana le Fay was done for the Champion Paper Company's "Pageantry" book. A large portrait of Merlin the Magician appeared on the opposite page, but I chose not to include it in this portfolio because it's too similar to the monk, and I like the monk better.

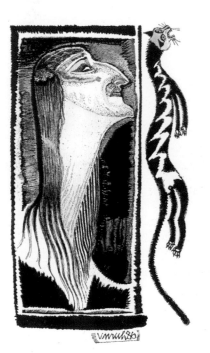

9. I think this piece makes a strong closing illustration. The portrait of Muddy Waters appeared in a recent issue of *Rolling Stone* magazine, and it ties in nicely with the opening pieces.

THE DESIGN FIRM'S PACKAGING PORTFOLIO

Jack Anderson from Hornall Anderson Design Works in Seattle, Washington, defines the particular presentation problems his firm encounters in his markets in this way: "Much of the business in our area tends to be more generalist in nature than what occurs back East, and presentations from our firm have to reflect this.

"When we present our credentials in a general sense, we speak to the fact that there are twenty-five people in our firm because we are working in five areas of related design. The five areas are identity, collateral (everything from small flyers to major brochures), packaging, environmental graphics (we are involved in a lot of signage and some exhibits and displays), and what we call promotion graphics, which includes calendars, posters, and very high-end invitations, which are often three dimensional. A sixth area that we have developed over the last couple of years is graphics in the sporting industry.

"We have some important decisions to make before a presentation. If this is a general review from someone who is not familiar with our firm and our work, we want to show them a little bit of all of us. The presentation will take one of two forms: a slide show or what we call portfolio boards. We have our dimensional work photographed and mounted on 18"x24" boards. We also mount some of our print work. Then we also bring a stack of collateral to pass around among those present during the meeting.

"The number of people at the meeting generally determines whether we present slides or boards, but in either situation, we use a lot of case histories. We try to document certain jobs, showing before and after. In that way, they can see the problem and our solutions, and it makes a very graphic impact. This shows them how we think and how we work. We frequently do a shotgun approach to all of the categories, and then do either one case history or three in specific areas that relate directly to the client. The message that I want to get across is that our firm is made up of a diverse group of people who don't do just one thing. We participate in all facets of design and I try to show this in our overall presentation."

Showing a packaging portfolio forces you to work with a great deal of physical dissimilarities in your presentation. In most cases it will be impossible for you to bring actual samples to a meeting. The smaller, less cumbersome examples are no problem, but a selection of skis or an assortment of food packaging will have to be photographed.

Jack has presented a selection of his packaging projects in portfolio form. The opening might be a title slide or a general piece to set the stage for the portfolio. "If I could show only ten images, I would show variety. I think a client needs to see that, and I can always present more of any segment," he says. This brief exposure to the projects will be enough to prompt questions and hopefully open the door to a more expansive presentation.

1.-3. This is such a success story, we have to open our presentation with it. The client needed a name, physical package identity, package design, and point of purchase display. Additional applications include a two slice promo/trial test package, bakery apron, coffee mug, buttons, banners and hats. We open with the product, then show the collateral, and close the section with the display.

Next we will go through a range of packaging projects, briefly explaining the assignment on each. We picked these specific projects because they represent such a broad product/client base.

4. The goal for this Seattle-based, fast-food chain was to design and implement the cafe's identity. Final applications included all paper food cartons and signage.

5. We created the logo and a unique visual image for the MicroSoft University's course collateral, which included packaging, calendars, binders, cassettes, and computer disks.

6. This jeans manufacturer wanted to project the up-scale quality and contemporary nature of its product. Final applications included rear pocket patch and hang-tag labels.

7. Our assignment was to recreate the feel of old-time grocery market service and high quality. A logo that combined traditional elements with the flair of contemporary retail attitudes was developed for application to letterhead, signage, aprons, bags, and multiple printed materials.

8. This boutique specializes in designer and antique jewelry. We developed an identity program, which was applied to the stationery, gift wrap, bags, signage and display-case treatments, and invitations.

9.-10. Diadora, an Italian athletic shoe manufacturer, wanted to increase its U.S. market share. Our graphic elements were used in package design for the shoe boxes and applied to product catalogs, T-shirts, sweatshirts, accessories, and athletic bags. In addition to the domestic shoe packaging, an international shoe box system was developed. A single black lid was used with four different boxes, one for each shoe type.

THE DESIGN FIRM'S CORPORATE IDENTITY PORTFOLIO

One of the best known design firms in the world today is Chermayeff & Geismar Associates of New York City. They employ a staff of approximately thirty-five, including professional architects and industrial designers as well as graphic designers.

"I think corporate identity is our strength because it is the one core which encompasses most of what we do," says partner Steff Geissbuhler. "We have done over 150 identity programs since the company formed in 1960." Among the clients for whom they developed trademarks and comprehensive identity programs are Mobil, Xerox, the Chase Manhattan Bank, the Museum of Modern Art, New York University, the U.S. Environmental Protection Agency, NBC, PBS, and the Rockefeller Center. They also designed the official American Revolution Bicentennial symbol.

Some of the identification programs are used in normal, expected applications. Other interpretations of identity programs are found in unlikely places. Frequently appearing in architectural appointments in an office building or television studio, or incorporated in a wall mural in an employee cafeteria, or as the public art on the sidewalk, the incarnations of corporate identity are thriving at Chermayeff & Geismar Associates.

In order for the design firm to show its impressive array of identities, a book was developed, using chronological order, to display the programs and occasionally some of the applications. The book is spiral bound in order to accept new work and the cover is a liquid crystal material that retains the imprint of whatever is pressed against it. "We thought it would be interesting if everyone who looks at it could leave their mark on the cover," explains Steff. "When we are called in on a corporate identity job, we bring the book and may use it as a leave-behind so that the client can study the work we've done."

Just as they tailor any presentation to the specific client, Chermayeff & Geismar Associates can closely focus an identity program to a specific industry. For a complete identity program, the design firm must be prepared to make several presentations to several levels at a corporation. The first meeting may be quite limited in what is pre-

sented. At each level, new material is added according to the information discovered at the previous meeting, and as an understanding of the client's particular design needs becomes apparent.

For this presentation, a selection of marks for the television industry was chosen. Rather than showing ten different marks, Steff chose to show five marks and examples of their applications. Since the marks aren't used in a vacuum, they weren't shown that way.

1.-2. We've chosen a small section of the firm's portfolio here, one which deals exclusively with our work in television broadcasting. We opened with the logo for the National Broadcasting Company because it is so widely recognized. The collateral material below shows only a small part of the logo application.

3.-4. We follow NBC with the logo and collateral for the Public Broadcasting Service, the national public television stations, because it is also nationally known. Together, they provide a strong opening and subliminally demonstrate the prestige of our clients.

5.-7. The program for WGBH Educational Foundation Channel 2, the Boston Public Television station, follows the national PBS logo and shows our work at the local level.

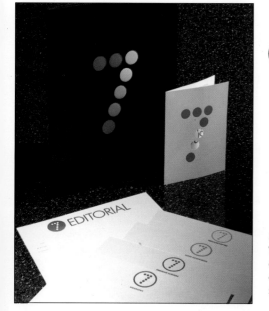

8.-9. We complement WGBH with Channel 7, one of Boston's commercial broadcast stations.

10.-11. We close this part of the portfolio with the program for Univision Holdings, Inc., the National Hispanic Television Network, our latest corporate identity.

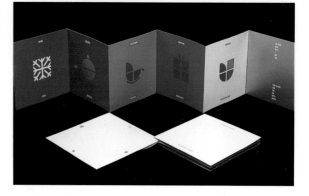

SEEKING FEEDBACK

You've now reached the point where your portfolio should be seen by eyes other than yours. The reason for seeking outside evaluation is to have someone whose judgment you trust reaffirm what you already know or at least suspect. Getting outside feedback on your work will be more important to you if you work on your own or if you're just starting out than if you are established or if you work with a group. It's also important if you're beginning a new direction in your work.

Even if you're just starting, you've already figured out that if you show your work to five different people, you will probably get five completely different reactions. How do you know who to believe? What if they hate it? Keep telling yourself, "This is not personal. This is one person's opinion about my work, not about me." After you've told yourself this, you must believe it.

HOW TO START

Look for the best people everywhere, and as you have an opportunity to travel around, write or call in advance of your arrival for appointments. If you're granted an appointment, be considerate of the opportunity and the person's time. For those people you can't personally visit, consider writing them a letter, telling them how much you admire their work, and include a promotional piece or something to introduce your work to them. If you're lucky enough to get a favorable response, follow up with a request to send your work to that person and ask for his or her critique.

HOW TO TAKE ACTION

Through the publications you read, you will become aware of the various conferences and shows held during the year that pertain to your field. Consider attending the one that is most suited to your work. You may not be able to get anyone to look at your portfolio there, but you can make contacts while exposing yourself to new ideas, techniques, and products in your industry. Some of the conferences you should consider attending are the Aspen Design Conference, On The Edge Conference, and the Park City Utah Conference (The Non Conference). Of course, many of the national organizations also sponsor conferences and workshops. Take advantage of your membership and attend.

If you're an illustrator, you may want to join the Graphic Artists Guild. Their handbook clearly presents information on business practices and pricing ranges that are invaluable to the experienced as well as the beginning illustrator. This book is chock-full of useful information, clearly written, and reasonably priced.

It seems the bigger the market you work in, the more impersonal it becomes. If you decide to show your book in Los Angeles or New York City, you will find people don't usually have a lot of time to spend with you, if they meet you at all. A drop-off policy is much more the norm. Unfortunately, so is limited feedback. Sometimes you will strike the perfect chemistry with someone who will be very helpful. But be prepared to go on a lot of interviews to find that person.

Choose these "evaluations mentors" carefully. First, they should be people whose work you know and whose opinions you will respect. Then you must listen to what they say. It's never easy to listen to criticism, even if it's constructive. But when you find someone you respect who is willing to offer it, consider yourself lucky, and use their comments to your best advantage.

Join clubs and subscribe to as many professional annuals and monthly magazines as you can afford. What you can't afford, locate in your local library and faithfully visit with each new arrival.

When he was president of the Art Directors Club of Dallas, Jack Summerford initiated a job fair, enabling graduating seniors from any college to bring in their portfolios and have them reviewed by local art directors from various advertising agencies and any corporations seeking entry level job applicants. Students from five states attended. Check with the art directors club in your area for club-sponsored portfolio reviews similar to this.

Be a joiner in your area. Get to know the people involved in your profession and take an active part in your local club so that they know who you are. It's important to maintain high visibility, especially if you're a newcomer. And if your clients are in the corporate community, you should seek an associate membership in those trade asssociations to which they belong. Many times it's easier to develop good business contacts in an informal setting rather than trying to get an appointment with a complete stranger.

Building relationships with people whose work you admire takes a long time. Like building a friendship, it is an investment. Friends are personal, peers are professional. Starting out or on a continuum, you need both.

MEET YOUR AUDIENCE

On the following pages are interviews with professionals who are in the business of looking at portfolios. They monitor the industry on a daily basis with an international eye, and they represent the toughest test of your portfolio—they are the people who assign the jobs. Even though portfolio reviews are only a part of their total responsibility, they know what they want to see, the presentation form best suited to their needs, and the suitability of the product to the market. The questions asked were directed primarily toward illustrators. The information in the answers is basic and applicable to designers and illustrators presenting a portfolio to any audience.

SPEAKING FROM EXPERIENCE
MELISSA GRIMES
Illustrator, Austin, Texas

Ask each person you call on to recommend other people you should show your portfolio to, especially when you're new to a market. This is an invaluable source of inside information—where there are openings, who hires a lot of freelancers, which are the best agencies or studios. It also gives you the opportunity to say "So-and-so suggested that I call you," which sometimes helps in getting appointments. In fact, when you assemble your first list of people to call on, don't necessarily use the phone directory. It lists everyone in town, but you want to target who's good and is a potential market for your work. That information is best found in national award annuals, art and design club mailing lists, and by word of mouth.

Pay attention to the reactions people have to the pieces in your portfolio. Do certain pieces always get good reactions? Do others never get a reaction? Solicit honest criticism from people you trust; ask them which piece they like best and why. Which piece would they leave out and why? Gauge the time it takes for someone to look through your portfolio. Do you sense their interest flagging at points? Maybe the presentation is too long. Reorganize your portfolio and watch for different reactions.

If your work doesn't sell in one marketplace, maybe it will in another. If you find yourself being uncomfortably typecast, you need to find visibility for your other work, even if you have to donate your services to get it published. Of course you shouldn't change your work solely on the basis of others' opinions. But you can't have tunnel vision either. Stick with the work you truly believe in, but try to see how it affects others.

Q&A: The Illustrator's Rep

A good representative can be a boon to an illustrator's career, but only when the timing is appropriate. Before you even consider approaching a rep, you must have gotten a few aspects of your career in order on your own. First, you have to have a body of work to show. Second, it is best that you show your work on your own for at least a year. Doing so will help you develop a necessary asset—a thick skin. This protective device will serve you well throughout your career.

Tony Andriulli, of Bernstein & Andriulli, Inc., in New York City, is one of the good guys in the business. He gets high marks from both artists and art directors. Although you may find some geographical differences, his organization's practices are fairly typical of representatives throughout the country.

What qualifications do you seek in an artist?

Aside from excellence, we want someone who has worked in the business for a while on their own. We feel it's necessary for most artists to show their own work, particularly at the start of their career because they need the feedback. If we insulate them against the real world, they will be working in a vacuum, and that's not doing anyone a service. Also, the artists need to have a chance to build up a body of work and to decide what kind of work they want to do.

What is your role as a representative?

We have several roles to fulfill. Our primary goal is to find those particular talents or styles that are apropos to our particular marketplace and bring that talent to that market. We have to find the talent and understand the market and the buying habits. We stay abreast of changes in personnel as well as styles. When we have found an artist whose work we think has potential, we try to guide them and help them tailor their work to the most commercial application. We try to match their portfolio to the needs of the marketplace.

What happens when you get a job ?

When the assignment comes in, we make sure it's the right kind of assignment; we negotiate the price, terms, conditions, and make sure the copyright is correct for the application. Then we bring the information to the artist, and he or she can accept or reject the assignment. If the job is accepted, we turn the artist over to the client. We stay close during each phase of production and act as a buffer so that the artist only has to worry about art. We try to keep our artists pure so they can talk on only a creative level. We want the artist to speak directly to the client about all aspects of the art. We want the client to speak to us about all aspects of the business. It takes all the pressure off the artist. We stay involved with the job all the way through and try to anticipate any problems that might arise and avoid them. We want to make this a pleasant experience for both our artist and the client.

Tony Andriulli

How do you show your artists' portfolios?

We have all the work shot on 8"x10" transparencies, which we shoot from the original art. We don't normally show the work in context. We mount each piece on a single 11"x14" black mat and file it.

Then when we get a call, we can put together a specific portfolio for the call. This is not a cheap way to show work, but it gives us the ability to custom design each presentation. By using the 8"x10" format, the work is shown in the best possible way and obviously we want our artists to look as good as they possibly can. Each artist is responsible for the costs of maintaining his portfolio. We keep a minimum of three complete portfolios for each of our artists, and that may consist of fifteen to thirty pieces. The numbers increase after they have been with us for a while.

How do you find the work?

You have to know the market and fit the right artist with the right client. When a call comes in, a book doesn't go out without one of us editing for that specific call. We ask questions of the people who call us. They tell us what they want to see and we give them more than they ask for.

Sometimes they know what they want to see and sometimes they don't. Sometimes they change their mind. We try to talk very candidly; it helps us to maintain a good relationship in the end.

How should an artist find the right agent?

They should ask questions. What is the track record of the agent, what is their taste level, how long have they been around? Talk to other artists. Decide what you want and if the agent can deliver. Some artists want to be kept closely informed, others don't want to hear from you unless you have a job for them. We run a business and try to tailor our methods to each artist as much as possible and stay 100 percent professional.

What is your commission rate?

Our split is 25 to 75 percent for the artists who are in New York City. For artists who are not in New York, we collect 30 percent, which we have to charge to cover the long distance aspect of our business. We also collect 30 percent on clients outside of New York for the same reason. We work on an open-ended contract stating that upon 30 days' written notice either of us has the right to cancel. The contract spells out exactly who is responsible for what and defines territories in the case of multiple representatives.

Do you handle billing for each job?

We send out the bills, do all of the collections, keep up with sales tax, return artwork—whatever policing actions are necessary. Generally, we take care of all of the financial arrangements of the job: estimates, expenses, whatever the job calls for. The invoices are paid to us, and we deduct our commission and pay the artist.

What kind of business do you seek for the artists you represent?

I would say that 35 percent of our business is advertising, 30 percent is corporate design and 35 percent is publication work, book jackets primarily. Advertising is still the top dollar in the illustration field, although some of the publication business pays quite well. Right now the romance novels pay the best of the publication work; last year it was the science fiction market. It changes depending on what's hot at the bookstores.

What kind of promotional schedule do you maintain for your clients?

A minimum of once a year national ads, direct mail in between. Usually we split the costs 25 percent to 75 percent unless we are sharing the ad with the artist's other representatives. Then the artist takes care of the cost.

Q&A: THE ADVERTISING AGENCY ART BUYER

Andrea Kaye from BBDO and Anna Solcz from J. Walter Thompson are both New York City-based art buyers. Once common only in the larger advertising agencies of New York or Los Angeles, this title is now found throughout the United States. The job was created because art directors didn't have the time to spend on areas other than creative. The poor use of art directors' time wasn't efficient and a lot of agencies were feeling client pressure for cost control. As you will see, there are some organizational differences between the agencies and preferences that are specific to each art buyer. But you will also see that they have more in common than not.

What is the function of an art buyer?

AK: To act as liaison between the agency and outside creative services such as illustrators, photographers, retouchers, and color houses. We are the purchasers of these outside services. We work internally with the creative and account management departments. With the creative department, we must understand what they want to get across creatively, and we assist them in terms of available talent who might work on a specific project. We must be familiar with specific talents across the country as well as around the world in a variety of disciplines. We also work with the account management people, who are interested in the cost of the talent. They are financially accountable directly to the client. We are the arbitrators between creative and financial; we are middlemen. We try to keep the job running smoothly, keep everybody happy and get the job accomplished properly.

Do you work for only specific art directors or for all of them?

AK: At BBDO we work with all of the art directors who work with print. We are assigned as a job comes up and we work on all accounts.

AS: At JWT we work on specific accounts with any art director who works on that account.

What happens when an artist has a first appointment with you?

AK: This may be a drop-off, possibly a personal interview. First, I want to check the suitability and quality level of the work, and after a few prelimi-

Anna Solcz (left) and Andrea Kaye (right)

nary questions over the phone, I can generally determine the experience level of an illustrator. I will try to spend five to ten minutes on a personal interview with someone I've never met before. That sounds brief, but that's really all the time I can spend. If we're talking about a specific job, we take as much time as we need. I want the illustrator to know something about us. Read *Advertising Age* or *Adweek* and find out what's going on in the business. I don't want to waste their time or mine. As an illustrator, I would seek out the work that I had the best chance at and call on that agency repeatedly. It may take a year or two, but you'll get in if your work is right.

AS: I don't like a drop-off policy. I like to meet the people I'm dealing with. Personalities are a big part of this job, and I want to know who I'm assigning. The chemistry is crucial, and I want the job to go smoothly. My policy is that an artist or a rep call and make an appointment. It may take a month or so to get one. My assistant makes my appointments and I see anyone. Once I've met you, I don't need to see you but once or twice a year unless there has been a drastic change in your style or your work in general.

What do you want to see in a book?

AK: First, remember that I am looking at it strictly from my viewpoint: What am I seeing that I can use at this agency on these clients? I can appreciate beautiful work on a personal level, but I have to look at the book in terms of what my needs are now or what they might be in the future. Then I focus on something that strikes me in the book and try to figure out a way to use it.

AS: I want to see a consistent style. I really don't look for diversity. I want to see a solid body of work, something that sets them apart from everyone else. You're competing against the best illustrators for some of the best jobs. I expect to see the best work.

Do you have any preferences in terms of the physical portfolio?

AK: The only thing that matters is whether the book is organized or disorganized. Time being what it is, I want something that is easy, compact, immaculate, quick to go through. I actually prefer mini-books; a book that I can look at at my desk, in my chair, under my light, at my telephone is a lot more appealing than something cumbersome. Large books sometimes put me off. I have limited space, so I must clear a space to open the book and possibly even go to another room. This book better be worth it.

Presentation is 50 percent of the portfolio. If the presentation is not good, then the work won't show well. I don't want to see more than twenty to twenty-five pieces. Almost no one shows slide trays anymore. We don't have a projector or a blank wall handy. The important thing is to come in, make a presentation, hopefully an impression and leave with a smile.

AS: I don't want to see a mini-book. I want to see something larger. I prefer 8"x10" chromes of the art, bound in a very neat presentation. I need to see ten to fifteen pieces that are consistently mounted. Sloppy portfolios turn me off. If someone's not proud enough of their work to make it neat and presentable, then I feel that's a reflection on how they are going to feel about a job. I don't like receiving a miscellaneous assortment of printed pieces or chromes in a brown envelope. I hate to present work to an art director in that form. The presentation really diminishes the quality of the work. Some days I have twenty-five books in my office. The sloppy ones will never make it. Also, slide trays don't go over big here. You can't drag an art director into a conference room to look at them. No one wants to take the time. If all you have is slides, put them in a plastic sheet.

What about leave-behinds and mailers?

AK: I keep what I like and I toss the rest. If I get something that's interesting and that I've never seen before, I call in the portfolio. I hate getting leave-behinds that are the same as what are found in the source books, and we use all the source books. Those go right in the garbage. If something in a source book has caught my eye, when I call in the portfolio I will mention that piece so the illustrator will know what I'm looking for. The leave-behind should be something visual, some way to remember the portfolio.

AS: I keep examples of all work I like. I receive mailings from all over the U.S., Canada, and Europe. I receive a lot of duplicate material that is in my source books, and I immediately trash that. When I come across a card that I like and it's not in my books, I hold on to it. I keep extensive files. My office is an extensions of my files, and sometimes it's pretty crazy in here. On my desk now, I have wind-up toys, a Mr. Machine, all kinds of products, lots of posters and photographs, dried flowers from someone. I also have lots of personal illustrations and other thoughtful items that artists have done for me as a thank-you.

Q&A: THE BOOK JACKET CREATIVE DIRECTOR

For illustrators, book covers are often the most rewarding assignments. There is usually minimal art direction; the pay falls somewhere between editorial and advertising, and there is the chance to produce award-winning art that may be viewed by literally thousands for years to come.

Publishers have in-house art staffs of varying sizes, but most of the cover work is assigned to outside illustrators. Each publishing house has various lines of books printed in different formats: hardbound books with and without dust jackets, and paperbacks. The fiction paperback can be one of the best-paying assignments, but the popularity of the market segment has a lot to do with the amount the publishing company can afford to spend on a cover illustration.

Jackie Merri Meyer is the vice president and creative director of Warner Books. She has worked in publishing thirteen years. Jackie is responsible for the art direction and design of book covers for Warner Books, Mysterious Press, Popular Library, and Little, Brown Paperbacks (a new mass-market line). She is one of the people responsible for how the mass-market titles look on the shelves of your bookstore today. Jackie will assign at least 350 covers a year, almost all of which use illustration.

Louise Fili was for eleven years the art director of Pantheon Books, a division of Random House in New York City. A widely respected book designer, Louise recently formed her own design firm. During the time she was with Pantheon, she assigned about 100 jackets a year on fiction and nonfiction, high-end publications. Now that she is on her own, she works with all kinds of books as well as other design projects.

Meyer and Fili represent two ends of the publishing spectrum but they have one thing in common. In order for your portfolio to be seen by them, it's going to have to be very good and it will probably get through the door only on the strength of your mailers.

What kind of portfolio policy do you have?

JMM: We have a drop-off only policy on Wednesday, and we pre-screen those by telephone. We probably get ten to fifteen calls a day for port-

folio reviews and we can't possibly see all of them. Six to ten books will arrive in our office each Wednesday morning, and during the day the staff will go through the books and leave their comments attached to each book. I go through the

Louise Fili (left) and Jackie Merri Meyer (right)

portfolios at the end of the day when I have some quiet time and can think about what I am seeing. I try to leave a note for every portfolio I review, indicating whether I want to see more samples, see it again in six months, or if it's unsuitable.

LF: Now that I'm on my own, I don't look at portfolios except on very rare occasions. Usually I call them in from a mailer I've received or from one of the sourcebooks I use. At Pantheon, I tried several methods, finally settling on a drop-off on the first Thursday of every month. My assistants would review the portfolios first, selecting the ones they knew I'd want to see. I'd keep those promos on file and ask those artists to keep in touch with me by mail only.

How do you most like to see portfolios?

JMM: I want to see what sets them apart from the hundreds of other illustrators there are out there. I want their work to show their sense of style, wit, and thinking. I see lots of work that is very mediocre and alike. To review the portfolios, I prefer to see tearsheets or mounted chromes. They should be easy to handle. The portfolio should have identification on the outside and a leave-behind on the inside with current address and telephone information already attached.

What kind of work do illustrators need to show to get publication work? Should they show only book covers?

JMM: Absolutely not. I want to see any work that reflects the illustrator's style. I want to see that their work is conceptual, not just decorative. It's also important that people put only their best work in their portfolio. If I see a book with nine great pieces and one piece that's bad, that's the one that I focus on.

If a book comes in with fifty samples, I'm going to make up my mind within the first ten samples and I may flip through the rest. But I think it shows a lack of confidence; ten to fifteen is a good number of samples.

LF: Illustrators should understand the publication business a little, do some homework. Go to bookstores and understand what is being done, who is art directing what, which covers you like and why, which covers you could do better and why. Then put together a cover portfolio aimed at solving real jacket concerns. If you're an illustrator and want to illustrate cookbooks, then you have to show food illustrations. It really is as simple as that.

What sourcebooks do you use?

JMM: I use the Society of Illustrators annual a lot. But I have all the sourcebooks and I use them all.

LF: I use *American Illustration* most commonly. I think it is the annual most suited to my taste. When I have a job that goes beyond that, something that is more unusual or more commercial, I usually look at *American Illustration Showcase* or the Society of Illustrators annual. Beyond that, my wall at Pantheon was entirely covered with artists' cards, promotions, and my own memorabilia, like one huge collage. Very often, all I had to do was look up at my wall and I was inspired.

What are your pet peeves about the process of hiring an illustrator?

JMM: People should know what kind of books we publish. If anyone is serious about doing work for a publishing house, they should have a copy of *The Literary Marketplace*. Don't expect me or my staff to educate you. Also, when they call to inquire as to our portfolio policy, it is not necessary to speak to the boss to get that information. My staff is competent and is certainly capable of relaying that kind of information.

LF: Attitude is everything. Some illustrators or reps can be extremely aggressive. Sometimes they don't want to leave the office until I give them a job. Professionals will understand that when the time is right, I will give them a call, and that can literally take years. Others feel that if they call me every day, I'll give them a job. That technique rarely succeeds in procuring work.

What about leave-behinds?

JMM: You have to use them. Without question, it's the way most of the jobs are assigned. I work with people from all over the world, and I keep extensive files. A once-a-year mailing is adequate. An illustrator asked me what I did with the mailers I receive. I told him, "The good ones I throw in the trash. The great ones I file." I refer to these files constantly and have called on artists seven or eight years after I received their mailer. Sometimes it takes that long for the right job to come up.

LF: I tell people the best way to keep in touch with me is through the mail. Two or three mailings per year is adequate, but they should be smart about when they send them out. You have to avoid the holiday season and the summer. Mailings could first go out after Labor Day, again in January, then early spring before everyone leaves for the summer. I don't think illustrators realize how much mail an art director receives. At Pantheon, I received two deliveries of mail a day, and it takes literally half an hour to go through each pile. After vacation, I would spend an entire day going through all the mailers. I threw away anything addressed to "Art Director." That's the same as "Occupant." It also doesn't hurt if you pronounce my name correctly.

RUDY HOGLUND

Q&A: THE MAGAZINE ART DIRECTOR

Since its inception, *Time* magazine has used illustration, and its cover has long been considered a prize among illustrators. Consequently, the art department receives literally hundreds of calls requesting portfolio reviews for inside spots as well as cover work. Rudy Hoglund has been the art director at *Time* for ten years.

What is the portfolio review process at **Time***?*

We have a drop-off only policy on Mondays and Tuesdays. Sometimes we accept portfolios on Wednesdays, but toward the end of the week our office gets busy putting the magazine to bed. We have at least one art director for each section in the magazine and they all assign their own illustration, and receive specific portfolios for that purpose. If I happen to see a portfolio I think would be good for one of the sections, I will send it to the specific art director. If you're a portrait artist, then I'm the one who should see your book.

It's necessary for illustrators to direct their portfolio to the appropriate art director. When artists call our department to set up a drop-off, they should be specific about what they are presenting and who should see it.

What do you want to see in a portfolio?

There is a level of quality I look for. Eighty percent of the work that comes in I'm not going to be able to use. Fundamental skills are certainly not the only criterion we use. When I look at a portfolio or mailer, I want to know that the illustrator has more than hand skills. A magazine cover has many tasks to fulfill, not the least of which is to illustrate the cover story. The portfolio must somehow demonstrate that this person can grasp ideas and interpret them in a form that is sophisticated, graphic, and creative. Also, be familiar with our magazine and the kind of illustration we use.

What about the physical presentation?

Neatness counts. If an artist has just thrown some work in a folder, it had better be good enough to impress me. I prefer to see the work in context to see the thought process behind the final illustration. I understand why illustrators want to show just the pure art. If they could show both on a page, we could both be happy.

What is a typical schedule for cover art?

It could be a month or two days. Nothing is typical on a weekly news magazine. Our stories change up until the last moment, and it's possible our covers will too. Sometimes it's possible to make a specific assignment ahead of time for, say, a holiday or a specific date, but many times our deadlines change and we must adjust quickly.

What guidelines do you give the illustrator?

Rudy Hoglund

First we find someone we think will have insight to the general topic, and if it's a portrait we talk about the posture of the subject, whether we want him or her worried or stately, pleased or whatever. We want to establish an attitude right off. If it's an idea, we may make suggestions or ask the illustrator to come up with something based on the reference material we provide.

What reference and sourcebooks do you use?

I probably use the annuals more than anything, including portfolios.

In the past, **Time** *assigned both photography and illustrative covers, sometimes in multiples. Is that still the case?*

Generally, I assign only one cover per week. Sometimes that rule is broken and we assign more than one illustration or an illustration and a photograph. We do this to cover two aspects of a story, but it is not the normal assignment pattern. Our covers almost always come before the story, but the cover has to reflect the final words. If the story changes, I may have to use photography because I no longer have time for illustration. I would say the ratio between photography and illustration is about 60 percent photography to 40 percent illustration.

SHOWING YOUR WORK

The best of all possible worlds is to show your portfolio in a one-on-one interview. In this situation, you have the chance to give your interviewer a good sense of yourself and your professional demeanor. You will also be able to find out about the person on the other side of the desk, to discover his or her likes and dislikes, and understand how you can improve your presentation with the person at the next interview.

A face-to-face meeting is a golden opportunity—don't blow it. Make sure that you're as well-directed, presented, and thought-out as your portfolio. If your book is neat and your appearance is not, the client is going to wonder which is the exception. Do your homework about the business of your prospective clients. Don't expect them to spend their time educating you about aspects of their business that are readily available.

SENDING YOUR BOOK ON A SAFE TRIP

When you comply with a potential client's drop-off policy, your portfolio has to stand on its own. Your initial phone call will determine what time to deliver the portfolio, and when it should be picked up. Generally it's a morning drop-off, and either an afternoon or next morning pickup.

Don't leave your portfolio longer than necessary. Once the review process has been completed, no one else will look at it and the chances of it getting lost increase. This is rare, but it happens. Keeping up with your book is your responsibility. If you can't collect it at the appointed time, call and make arrangements for it to stay longer; tell the client exactly when you will pick it up, and get the name of the person you speak with.

If you use a delivery service, keep up with the reference numbers for each delivery and pickup. Get the service's policy on loss or damage ahead of time. Normally, if you make the call to have your book reviewed, you pay the delivery charges. If your book is called in, the caller may take care of it.

If you send your portfolio out of town via courier service, keep your receipts. If you need additional insurance, be sure to indicate the amount for the return trip. Pack your portfolio adequately to protect it from damage.

The outside of your portfolio should be clean and clearly marked. It's a good idea to have either

Always keep in mind that you are in the graphic communications business. Your portfolio is communicating with professionals within that same world. Present your portfolio as if each piece were the Hope Diamond. Be proud of it. Be enthusiastic about it. If you're not, who will be? Let the clients know that you want to work with them, and ask for the opportunity.

Listen carefully to their criticism as well as their praise. Watch where they pause and notice which pieces attract their attention the most. After you leave, make a few notes on the interview—something you can refer to at your next opportunity. If it's appropriate, follow up with a note or a quick drawing of some topic you discussed during the interview. Interviewing is not a spectator sport. You have to have participation from both sides, so take this time to capture their interest.

your business card or your mailing label laminated, with an extra inch of lamination added to the left-hand side. Attach the laminated tag to the case with a leather strap, such as those found on luggage tags. Attach an identification card that cannot be removed to the inside of your case as well. In a side pocket, pack a list of the contents of your portfolio, especially if it is not in a bound form. Keep it current and keep a copy. Be sure to list any extras you include, like tearsheets and samples.

If you have an unbound portfolio, consider numbering each board. Not only will this help you to control the order in which your work is viewed, but it will be easier to keep up with the individual pieces. It's not a bad idea to put an identification sticker or business card on the back of each piece. Sometimes, art directors will pull work they like from various portfolios and make photocopies. It's possible they could put it back in the wrong portfolio.

Every time your book comes back, check it for contents, order, and anything that doesn't belong in it. If you use laminations, you should check to see if they need cleaning or polishing. The same goes for acetate sleeves. Your portfolio should never be shown in less than pristine form, and you should always be prepared to send it out on a moment's notice.

PRESENTING YOUR WORK

Think of choosing the proper presentation form for your portfolio in the same way you would choose a bottle of wine to accompany your dinner. The best choice will enhance its accompaniments; the tastes will be compatible and the combination should improve the entire experience.

The presentation of your work will account for half of the overall impression. That's because you're showing a graphic product to a graphic consumer. The key word here is *graphic.* To some degree, everyone who sees your work is making decisions based on visual input.

OPTIONS FOR MOUNTING YOUR WORK

After you decide which pieces to use, you must decide how to show them. You have lots of options: 35mm, 4"x5" and 8"x10" transparencies, printed samples mounted various ways, laminations, actual pieces mounted or sleeved. If you're showing your work to a group and don't want to use 35mm slides and a projector, mounting printed work on large foam-core boards for an easel or a freestanding display is a possibility. This is a good way to show a series of spreads or before-and-after comparisons. Posters or dimensional work are less awkward to transport and display when photographed and shown in transparency form.

Laminations are yet another option. They provide permanent protection for samples, and may be ordered in various thicknesses, with several styles of finishes. The disadvantage of using laminations is that they easily become scratched. They are also heavier than other mounting materials, so if you frequently send your portfolio by mail or an express service, laminations will add to the cost.

Mounting tearsheets or transparencies, either 4"x5" or 8"x10", is a common presentation method for illustrators who prefer an unbound portfolio. The advantage here is flexibility. You choose the pieces to include and order them in the most appropriate way for a specific call. The disadvantage is that you must keep up with all the loose pieces and see that they are returned.

The bound portfolio case takes the most editing consideration, since you see a spread each time you flip a page, and the facing pieces must work together. The disadvantage of the bound book is a lack of flexibility. Even if you use only right-hand

Your work is likely to be perceived in the same manner it is presented; so present it with confidence, enthusiasm, and perhaps a touch of reverence. Think about how a fine jewelry store shows a diamond necklace. They don't pull it out of the case and hand it to you. The salesperson arranges the necklace on a velvet background designed to enhance the brilliance of the creation. Would you do less with your own work? Whether the presentation is to a corporate client, an art buyer, or is a drop-off at a potential client's office, the goal is the same. Presentation cannot be ignored.

pages, you have to take the book apart to change or add new pieces. If you use both right- and left-hand pages, the job becomes more complicated.

Whatever your choice of case, bound or unbound, you have the options of size and color to consider. To some extent the size you choose will depend on your budget. The larger the format, the more expensive the production and transportation costs. If you show your work locally, this may not be a problem (but keep in mind that you still have to lug it from place to place). If you plan to ship it across the country, either develop two formats or keep the size relatively small. The size of the standard express box is 12½"x17½"x3".

Look at your work mounted in 4"x5" format as well as 8"x10" or 11"x14" and decide which format most enhances your work. Does it lose impact in the smaller size, or does your style lend itself to the more intimate format? What is the nature of the work you're showing? Does it need more space around it? Is the proportion better with larger work and smaller mat? Are you showing it in context or not? Will the size accommodate both your horizontal and vertical pieces?

Next you must decide on the color of the mounts. Unless you are showing only black-and-white work, it will be difficult to use any strong colors as a background. The most likely choices will be black, white, or some shade of neutral gray. Black is the most commonly used and the most resistant to showing wear. White is the most fragile. Gray can add a warmer, less stark feeling. Your final decision is based on the specific work you are showing and how it looks best.

The proportion and the color of the mount will affect the visual presentation of your work. Shown opposite is the same piece mounted in 8"x10" size on an 11"x14" mount (top row); 4"x5" size on an 8"x10" mount (center row); and two 4"x5" pieces on a single 11"x14" mount (bottom row).

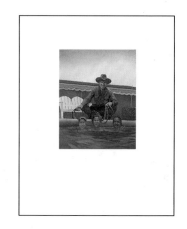

WORKING WITH A PROJECTOR

If a 35mm slide tray is the format for your presentation, you must add two elements of chance to your list of considerations. Always call ahead to ensure that the client has an appropriate place for the slide tray to be viewed. Next, add the element of mechanical failure. Nothing is worse than appearing before an audience expecting to see a slide presentation with nothing to show. If the airline lost your tray or the bulb burned out after the second slide, you have a forty-five-minute ad-lib to deliver instead of a terrific visual presentation.

To diminish that possibility, there are some precautions to take. For starters, always keep your slide tray with you. Don't check it as luggage on an airline. If you send it ahead, send it far enough in advance that you can be assured of its safe arrival before you yourself have left your office. Keep a set of dupes. Never send out originals. If you are doing a really important slide presenta-tion, use glass-mounted slides—they have to defy gravity to stick in the projector. If you are using someone else's projector, arrive early enough to try out the projector and make sure it works to your satisfaction. If the operator tells you that most of the time you have to double click the button to get the slide to advance, strongly consider finding another projector. Make sure there are spare bulbs at hand. If you have any doubts about the equipment, bring your own. You will be rewarded for your trouble. Number each slide on a consistent corner so the person loading the tray will arrange them correctly.

If you've sent a sheet of slides as an adjunct to your portfolio, make sure each slide is marked with your name. The prospective client may load your slides in a tray with other work. It also helps if you give the client a written description of the slides you send.

A case for a carousel slide tray, custom-designed by Brewer-Cantelmo, a New York City firm that has been making portfolio cases for over sixty years. This case is available in larger sizes that will accommodate additional trays. Check with your local photographic supply stores to see the various kinds of cases available.

HOW MANY PORTFOLIOS SHOULD YOU HAVE?

Ideally, you should be prepared with the following:

- One for drop-off (gone for the day, designed to stand on its own).

- One for yourself (to keep at the office in case of a drop-in and as a backup).

- One to leave with a client (gone for an undetermined period of time).

- One for mailing out (with appropriate packaging for a safe trip).

Carrying cases come in a variety of sizes and prices, and should be used to protect your portfolio. Ideally, the two should be purchased together. Be sure to pay particular attention to how waterproof the case is, as well as to the durability of the zipper, handles, and straps. (Special thanks to Sam Flax for providing these cases and other items from their line of presentation materials for this book. And special thanks to Brewer-Cantelmo for providing items from their line also.)

Books may be bound with a screwpost or metal spine, as well as ring binders. Sheet protectors are available in acetate, vinyl, or mylar. The heat and humidity in your location may have a bearing on your choice of materials. Ask the most knowledgeable person at the art store which is most appropriate for your needs. (Above) This leather folder and case with acetate sleeves is best for a longer-than-average presentation. This particular case comes with the option of screw-post or spiral binding. Similar items should also be available from your local art supply store. (Right) This Brewer-Cantelmo Tear Sheet Book can be customized to any size and thickness. It is shown here with its black nylon carrying case. This rain-proof, padded carrying case protects the leather of the binder and prolongs the life of the portfolio.

THE ULTIMATE PORTFOLIO

(Right) A clam shell storage box, with carrying case, is intended for a presentation made up of loose pieces, either mounted or laminated. If you use these boxes as a storage system for your art, be sure they are lined with acid-free paper. This box has an unhinged 2" gusset which allows the box to open 180 degrees. (Below) Storage or mailing tubes for architectural drawings or poster transportation. The red tubes, available in several sizes, are expandable plastic suitable for smaller quantities of art. The large black tube has the largest opening and has a heavier construction than the others. Both have straps for carrying ease. (Bottom right) A leather attaché case, available in several sizes, may carry either your book or loose mounted pieces. Additional support materials and leave-behinds can be kept in a side pocket of the case.

Shown here are three variations from the Elegánte and Traygánte series from Brewer-Cantelmo. This book/box combination features a flap, handle and screwpost binding. Each book can be custom-stamped with your name or logo. Although this exact item may not be available, similar ones may be found in your local art supply store.

The Sorel portfolio, a two-flap, lightweight box folder, is designed for twelve to eighteen square laminations or mounts, and can display your work both horizontally and vertically. The carrying case is separate. Buy the best presentation materials you can afford. How your package looks may determine whether it gets opened.

These two Presentation Mailers are a lightweight answer to air express portfolios. The larger box on the bottom fits perfectly in a standard air express shipping carton. The wooden sides provide support and help protect your art when it leaves the safety of your office.

You can make up portfolios to be mailed, or entire graphic presentations with this system. The folders can be color coded for easy identification and the entire system, including the folder and the envelope, are available in air express size. Sam Flax offers this presentation system in several sizes and colors. Check out what's available at your art supply store. If they don't have a particular item, they can often order it for you. (Or you can try mail order supply houses yourself.)

These lightweight carrying cases are made of corrugated plastic, and come in a variety of sizes. They can handle anything from a video cassette up to legal-sized documents.

VIDEO CASSETTES

The leading edge form of portfolio is the video cassette. Illustrator Dave Jonason is beginning to experiment with this format because, as he says, "I'm also working in television computer art with Quantel Paint Box, and I see this as the next phase of my art to develop. I think computers are the tool of the future, and television is a natural medium for this tool. Animations and computer-generated art will have broad applications. I think portfolios in the form of video cassettes will certainly happen."

Keep in mind his use of the word *will.* This is still an unusual format, and you can't expect everyone to be prepared for it. If your prospective client doesn't have the capability to view the cassette, you're out of luck. This is one obvious disadvantage of the format. Another disadvantage is price. The cost of producing a seven-minute video on cassette will range from $2,500 to $10,000, depending on in-house capabilities, lighting, locations, music, and talent.

However, the portability is a real advantage for someone doing lots of out-of-state assignments. Video can also be very well-suited to environmental or exhibition work, work that's hard to show in transparency form. As with slides, never send out the master tape—always keep that in a safe place—and use dupes for the presentations.

LEAVE-BEHINDS AND OTHER PROMOTIONAL MATERIALS

Promotional material may get your portfolio in the door more often than you realize. Your leave-behinds are a key to getting your portfolio shown when you couldn't get a phone call returned. It is essential that you use some form of mailing and that continuity exists between these leave-behinds and your portfolio.

Your promotional material must stand out among a formidable crowd. Think about the stack of mail an art director or an art buyer receives each day. If the mailer is properly addressed, then you have a chance that it will be opened by the intended party. At that moment, the decision will be made to file it, pin it up on the wall, or toss it into the trash. It's just that simple and just that quick. Once your piece is filed, it may stay there for years. If you move or get a new rep, send an update announcing the change.

PROMOTIONAL MATERIAL FOR DESIGNERS

Designers and design firms don't normally use reps or page listings in sourcebooks. They have to devise other ways to tell the world about themselves and their services. Most commonly, they produce either a brochure or book of their work. Some may engage a public relations firm to find local or national publicity. Almost all design firms give a party at least once a year to which they invite both existing and prospective clients.

Since most design work is done for corporations, promotional material must be targeted to that audience. Promotional pieces for designers come in many forms. Some use brochures to show a range of work produced by their firm; others choose a single job and use it as a successful case history. Lots of designers have published a book on their work and use that as a leave-behind. Some books are small and precious. Others are large and impressive. Almost anything goes.

Designers must enjoy Christmas more than any other season, judging from the party invitations and cards they send out. Some send gifts as well. Firms often take advantage of holidays to thank their old clients and invite prospective clients in to see their offices and meet their staff. A move to a new location or the celebration of a notable award or even the first appearance of spring is a good enough excuse for a gathering. Designers can use the opportunity to create imaginative invitations and theme decorations for their celebration.

On these pages you'll find a selection of successful promotions used by designers across the country. They show a wide range of styles and purposes. Use them as a starting point for your own imagination, and think about how you can promote your own business in a special and personal way. Do you have a spectacular or unusual office space? Use it to a more public advantage and let it become part of your signature. Is there a local event that occurs each year in your area? Perhaps you can arrange a promotion to tie into it. Make your promotions as memorable as possible, but keep your audience in mind. Whatever your effort, it should reflect your own style and be appropriate to the type of work you seek.

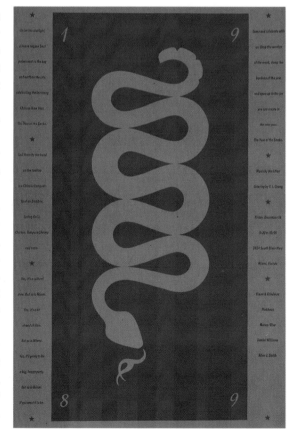

Pinkhaus Design of Miami uses their spectacular building to host a yearly holiday celebration. The theme is announced not only through the invitations, but on flags specially designed for the occasion.

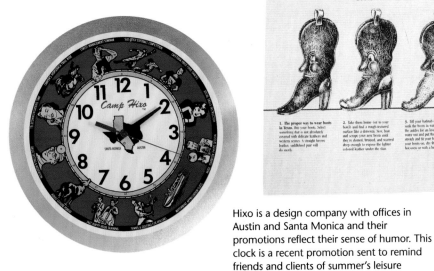

Hixo is a design company with offices in Austin and Santa Monica and their promotions reflect their sense of humor. This clock is a recent promotion sent to remind friends and clients of summer's leisure activities. (Right) *How To Be Texan*, a book designed and written by Hixo, and published by Workman Press, is also used as the firm's general promotion and leave-behind.

Pentagram/San Francisco designed this "Pentagram Papers" on Chairman Mao political buttons. This is one in a continuing series of small brochures periodically produced by the firm's various offices, and is but one facet of the firm's promotional activities.

An invitation to a Pinkhaus Design rooftop party.

Morla Design of San Francisco made use of label and package design work they did by sending out gift boxes of candy to their holiday list. Recipients could enjoy the candy as well as the design—a clever way to be remembered.

PROMOTIONAL MATERIAL FOR ILLUSTRATORS

If you're an illustrator using more than one style, don't send multiple styles out on the same promotional piece. You'll confuse your audience. Here are a few tips to increase the survival rate of your promotional material.

- Figure out an annual marketing/promotions budget. This should include the production and mailing of your promotional pieces, along with any advertising, including source books and perhaps show entries. Plan your mailings ahead and print several at once to reduce costs.

- Make sure your name and telephone number, or those of your rep, are correct and readable.

- Your mailer should be properly and personally addressed. Avoid sending out mailings addressed to "Art Director." Update your mailing list at least once a year, more often if possible. People change jobs a lot. Watch the trade publications for updates on who's moved and where targeted business has gone.

- Think of your promotional piece the same way you would think of developing a billboard on the highway. You must make visual impact in less than ten seconds. Use only work that represents the style in which you're comfortable. Don't send out a specialty piece—even if it turned out well—unless that's the kind of work you want to pursue.

- Consider doing special, personalized pieces for certain people. You can't do this on a large scale, but for special art directors it may be worth it.

- Don't forget holidays. Use the festive mood to send a supplemental greeting (and reminder of your work).

- Plan your mailings by your clients' schedules. If they leave town each summer, don't send mailings in their absence. Know roughly the busy and the slack periods. Time your mailings to arrive just before things get busy.

- Don't send out a huge mailing all at once. Stagger it. You don't want to have to turn down work because you're too busy, only to sit idle a month later, waiting for the phone to ring.

- Do at least one mailing that is not the same as your sourcebook advertising. Those who use the sourcebooks tend to discard identical pieces.

- Make a list of specific targets for each market you want to cover. Keep a list of the responses you received and place them on an "active" list.

- Don't forget trade associations and in-house publications that use illustration.

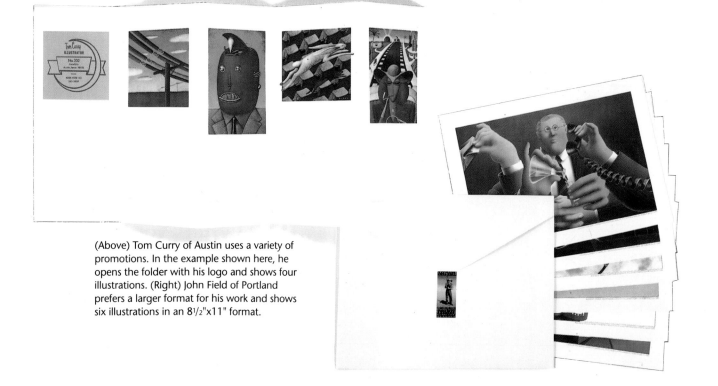

(Above) Tom Curry of Austin uses a variety of promotions. In the example shown here, he opens the folder with his logo and shows four illustrations. (Right) John Field of Portland prefers a larger format for his work and shows six illustrations in an 8½"x11" format.

Hungry Dog of Atlanta had T-shirts made up for an exhibition of their art at the Urban Lounge in Nashville.

(Above) Norman Green of West Redding, Connecticut, used his award-winning illustration as the basis for a self-promotion. On the back fold is the name and address for his representative. (Left) Jack Unruh of Dallas did a series of illustrations for an annual report. He selected the images he wanted to use as a promotion and spiral-bound them into a small book, with an original cover and back page.

TEN PROFESSIONAL PRESENTATIONS

In this final section sample portfolios are presented from designers and illustrators from across the country. Every effort was made to reproduce their work in the same manner they prefer to show it. They have been more than generous in sharing not only their artwork, but also their thoughts on how and why they make their presentations in this manner.

The majority of these portfolios are from some of the country's top professionals, yet their methodology should be no different than yours. You'll find they often share the same concerns you will have in choosing which pieces appear in your portfolio and ultimately, their portfolios have the same purpose as yours will—getting the right job from the right client.

This section presents a diverse selection of work and working situations, ranging from the rather involved presentations of large design groups to the more straightforward presentations of the illustrator. Each professional was asked to submit a portfolio for a particular assignment, and they have tailored their presentations to specific requests.

The exceptions in this section are the two opening portfolios, which belong to students from Art Center College of Design in Pasadena, California. The design portfolio comes from a fifth-term student, and the illustration portfolio is an example from a graduating student. These portfolios serve as benchmarks, showing the formation and the finished portfolios, which are really only a beginning to the professional world.

The professional design firms were asked to prepare a presentation for a corporate client rather than for an advertising agency. While the request was the same, each of the design groups has a different slant to their books, reflecting the specific kind of work they want to solicit from a potential source.

The portfolios shown in this section come not only from various parts of the country, but also from firms that vary greatly in their size. From Communication Arts in Boulder, Colorado, with forty seven people, to Jack Summerford in Dallas, Texas, who runs a single-person office, great work comes from all quarters and in large and small packages.

Some of the illustrators represented incorporate their illustration only in the context of their own design. Their portfolio becomes an amalgam of design and illustration. In other cases, the illustrators are individuals working alone or sharing office space. In the rather unusual case of Hungry Dog Studio of Atlanta, Georgia, a husband and wife team show both their individual work as well as their collaborative work.

The portfolios that follow represent not only the work of your competition, but also of your colleagues. You'll find situations that apply directly to your own work, gain new insight into related areas, and learn presentation techniques that will enable you to polish your own performance for your clients.

ART CENTER
COLLEGE OF DESIGN

In 1930 a young advertising man, Edward A. "Tink" Adams, saw growing opportunities for designers in the flourishing magazine and newspaper industries and in the burgeoning field of industrial design, but no existing school was preparing artists for entry into the business world.

Adams opened Art Center School in downtown Los Angeles. From twelve faculty members and eight students working out of makeshift headquarters, Art Center College of Design now occupies a 166,000-square-foot steel and glass structure located on 175 acres that overlook Pasadena's Rose Bowl. Its faculty numbers more than 200 and its full-time enrollment of 1,200 students represents virtually every state and some thirty countries. An additional 400 students are enrolled in Art Center's evening program.

The college's purpose has been remarkably consistent. Art Center remains dedicated to developing in its students the strong technical foundation and conceptual ability required by the clients, industries, and organizations that eventually employ them. Moreover, the college recognized the broader role the designer occupies in today's economy and is dedicated to offering a comprehensive program that addresses the total needs of the emerging designer, art director, illustrator, photographer, filmmaker, or painter. In 1986, the college opened an affiliate campus in a nineteenth-century chateau near Vevey, Switzerland.

THE DESIGN STUDENT'S PORTFOLIO

James Miho, chairman of the Graphic and Packaging Design department, shares his insights on portfolio development and presentation:

"The portfolio is the map of student work from first term to eighth term. Everyone talks about concepts and ideas, but few can actually do it. I like to encourage students to incorporate something special in their ideas, and that is their own cultural strength. There are thirty-three countries represented here at Art Center, and more at our Swiss campus. The results of all this cultural cross communication are amazing. We look at portfolios in Europe, Asia, and America. Different countries have different solutions. Annie Huang's fifth term portfolio (pages 80-81) is one of many.

"We accept admission portfolios on a year-round basis. In my department alone (which is one of nine departments), we review about 300 each year and accept 5 to 10 percent. Each of the books is reviewed by at least two department staff members. We are looking for possibilities, students who show promise and imagination. They may present their portfolios in any form they choose, and the content varies quite a bit. Once the student is accepted, we don't worry about a formal portfolio until a formal review in the fifth term in this department. We review the progress of each student on a personal basis from the first to the fifth term to help them discover their strengths and weaknesses. We want to help them along. It is also a good gauge for the level of instruction the students receive. We can tell what students are learning from what appears in their work. We look at notebooks, roughs, sketchbooks, and preliminary drawings as well as finished pieces in order to see how the student arrived at a particular solution. Then we can understand the validity of the problem as well as the validity of the solution. The only exception to this schedule are scholarship students, and their portfolios are reviewed each term.

"At the middle of the eighth term, which is the final term, the student receives a formal portfolio class. We hold portfolio classes for about a week and work individually with each student. We talk about what they want to do and where they want to live and what salary they want to earn. We try to expose them to international situations and help them think in the broadest terms. Then we teach them how to focus on specifics and direct their portfolio to their chosen market.

"By the end of March, the graduating student has his or her final portfolio in shape. April is recruiting month on campus. We have representatives from major corporations, headhunters, and design firms from around the world. They hold interviews with students who set up appointments and present their portfolios. About 85 percent of our graduating students have jobs when they leave Art Center.

"Transparencies and original art are the normal format. We suggest they use 8"x10" transparencies, and if the student has packaging or outsized art, then those should be photographed. We make a specific effort to show typography in a design portfolio. We have both Europeans and Americans teaching typography, and we want our students to understand each perspective. We teach with both hot type and computers so the students first learn hand-set then the Macintosh. We interface typography with learning systems so it becomes part of each student's graphic vocabulary."

THE ILLUSTRATION STUDENT'S PORTFOLIO

Philip Hays, Chairman of Art Center's Illustration Department, offers the following thoughts on the content and presentation of a graduate's portfolio:

"Alexey Brodovitch, the legendary art director of Harper's Bazaar, gave out assignments with the admonition, 'Astonish me.' I would give the same advice to the graduate student in preparing a portfolio. When a student addresses me with the familiar question, 'What should I put in my graduate portfolio?' my answer to them invariably is, 'Whatever it is that you most love to do.'

"However, there are practical considerations in the preparation and final selection of a graduate portfolio. First and foremost is that the work included should address the market in which the graduate is going to seek employment. This applies to the kind or kinds of illustration (editorial, advertising, book, children's book, fashion, and the many other less-defined work places for illustration) and also to the geographic location. The type of work available varies a great deal in different parts of the country, both nationally and internationally. There is another consideration: Is the graduate planning a career as a freelance illustrator, as most are, or seeking steady employment?

"A graduate student seeking employment should include preliminaries, such as initial thumbnails and sketches, comps, working drawings, and finished art. This shows work habits and thought processes and is of great interest to a future employer.

"The graduate seeking freelance work should not include preliminaries. An art director looking at freelance portfolios is interested only in the final result and does not care how it came to be. This portfolio should contain only finished art that speaks for itself. Some of these students do put the work into layout form, complete with captions and headlines, if this helps to clarify the concept.

"Portfolios should, of course, be well organized, clean, and as compact as possible. For large art, an 8"x10" transparency is usually the best answer. Small original art should be shrink-wrapped for protection. Many art directors have a drop-off policy. I recommend a portfolio made up entirely of 8"x10" and 4"x5" transparencies for drop-off.

"The portfolio should contain a promotion piece showing a striking image, name, address, and telephone number to be left with the art director. If the graduate cannot afford to have these printed, a color photocopy or C print with a business card attached will do in the beginning.

"The work included should be fresh, personal, and creative. Individuality should be stressed. It is against the professional portfolio that the student will be competing. A graduate portfolio should be more exciting than that of a professional because a student has the freedom to make it so. I tell my students to seize the opportunity."

ANNIE HUANG

Annie Huang is a fifth term student at Art Center. The work shown on these pages reflects her portfolio at this stage in her student career. The complete Art Center program is eight terms, at which point a graduate portfolio is developed. She doesn't have a lot of work to show yet, so she arranged it for aesthetic appeal on the page.

The assignment was to design a complete identity program for Diaghilev, The Art of Enchantment exhibition. This program consists of a folder, bag, program guide, invitation, and a watch designed for the time of event, which was given to patrons at the event.

This prototype was the response to an assignment to develop an educational tool for cultural awareness that would interface with a laser disk player. This unit is designed to be a portable teaching tool for children. A query from one of the selected categories produces an answer on the screen.

The assignment was to develop a new passport for a country. In this case, Germany was chosen as the country and a smaller format (more compatible with EEC guidelines) was designed, with international computer interface abilities.

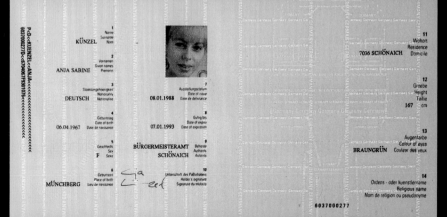

MARC BURCKHARDT

Marc Burckhardt presents his graduate illustration portfolio from Art Center. He included a wide range of work to show he can do all types of illustration. He has since moved to New York City to begin his career. In six months to a year, he will have completely changed his portfolio, adding printed work and beginning to reflect his chosen specialty.

The assignment was to produce an illustration for an existing campaign that showed a sense of humor. The headline for this ad reads "Milk for an active life."

In promoting a solar-powered vehicle race, this poster was developed to raise awareness among high school and college level students and promote the aspects of solar power rather than the actual race.

An annual report cover for the
management division of a financial
institution, this assignment is
directed to corporate and editorial
work rather than advertising.

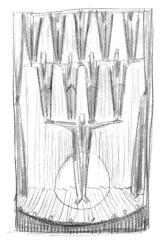

THE ULTIMATE PORTFOLIO

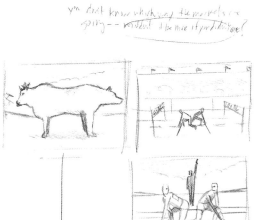

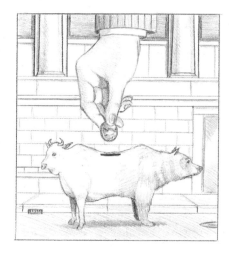

The assignment was to use an existing campaign and headline and give it a conceptually appropriate image.

Using liquor as the product, the assignment was to produce an image-oriented ad. The image is meant to elicit strong feelings of the Southwest and cowboy era.

GOLDEN GATE

NITE TIME

HERBAL TEA

Created for an advertising class,
this was the response to the problem of developing a product label

RUNYAN/HINSCHE ASSOCIATES

The year 1959 was a landmark in the design world. Until then, annual reports were mostly an organized collection of numbers distributed to stockholders and investors. Robert Miles Runyan, backed by his client Litton Industries, decided to change all that. Runyan didn't set out to revolutionize the annual report, he just wanted to make it better, really the best. And the 1959 Litton annual report was just that. His use of type and photography not only changed the way annual reports look, but opened corporate doors to an expanded world of design. Corporations redefined the purpose and look of all their collateral work.

According to Gary Hinsche, Runyan/Hinsche Associates believes a good portfolio is made up of great work—solid, innovative graphic design.

"That's been our goal since the firm was formed in 1955. We're one of the oldest graphic design firms in the United States, and it gives us an extraordinary range and depth of work to show.

"An occasional good project isn't nearly as provocative as year after year of solid design for a diversified client base. And our consistent performance has attracted some of the finest design talent in the field. We maintain a staff of about twelve people.

"Whether you're showing your work to a prospective client or your peers at a design association meeting, the presentation is a form of portfolio review. We constantly collect the best examples of our work to use in our presentations. It's an ongoing assignment.

"Routinely, we record most of our projects on 35mm. Our work is reviewed at least twice per calendar year and and we determine which pieces we want to record on an 8"x10" format. We also maintain a supply of printed samples.

"Bob Runyan, Michellene Griffin and I are responsible for presenting RHA's portfolio. We usually make 90 percent of the company's new business calls. Currently, we make five to ten presentations a week.

"For this book, we were asked to assemble a presentation for annual report work. In a way, an annual report is like a corporate portfolio. It is a document carefully directed to a specific market, graphically presenting a company's achievements.

(From left) Robert Miles Runyan and Gary Hinsche

"Our portfolio is structured to fit the prospective client. The type of work the prospect is seeking and the industry they represent are factors that influence what goes into the portfolio. Many of our presentations require a combination of the three formats: slides, 8"x10" transparencies, and actual printed samples.

"For an annual report presentation, we won't just show annual reports. First, we want the client to understand that we do a lot more than that. As we show each piece, we will point out aspects of other assignments reflected in each piece. For instance, a corporate identity, or store front design used in the report.

"We also like to show some spreads or art out of context rather than the standard cover and spread shot. This gives us a chance to open a dialogue with our prospective clients and draw them into the presentation. Of course, we always have the actual book to show them a complete piece to back up the visual.

"We choose the specific examples because they represent a variety of design solutions. One of the points we make during the presentation is that we don't have a 'look.' We try to approach each annual report from a fresh standpoint, so our presentation reflects this diversity. I don't like long presentations and I don't think you have to show a lot of work in order for a prospective client to get a feel of the quality level he may expect."

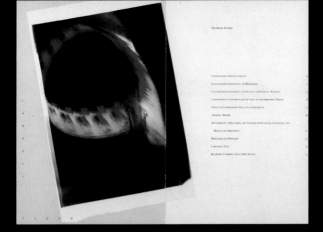

A spread from the Compact Video, Inc. 1985 Annual Report.
The close relationship between the client and the designer
resulted in a book with vivid colors and images drawn from the
firm's technology and products to complement that message.

An inside spread from *Optimum Care* magazine. Obviously this piece
and the one that follows aren't annual reports, but we want to
diversify the presentation and frequently use examples like these.

Exhibition design for Norman Foster, Foster 10 Architect, Tokyo

Dell Computer Corporation Annual Report, 1990. We show the cover art only.
This is one of the opportunities to discuss how the art was used throughout the
book and what an honor it was to be chosen to do their first annual report.

First Los Angeles Bank Annual Report 1988, inside spread art. This book is a terrific example of how beautiful black- and-white can be. Budgets are always a concern, and we want to show that we can keep a high-quality look while remaining mindful of budget considerations.

Nichols Institute Annual Report 1987 inside spread. This is one of the most award-winning annual reports we've ever done.

Times Mirror Annual Report 1988. An inside page and spread from the report. We particularly like the dimensional graphs shown in this book. This communications company is very well known and maintains a high profile. It's a strong piece to use to close the presentation.

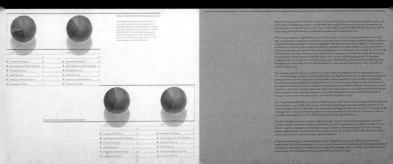

JACK SUMMERFORD DESIGN

"I thought about hiring a receptionist, but then that would double my staff. And once I started growing, where would it stop? Would I have to hire junior designers and bookkeepers? Would I have to move to an office with more space? The idea of growing just for growth's sake seemed to cause more problems than solutions.

"I like working closely with my clients. There's less chance of misinterpretation and mistakes. They like it, too. I like not having scheduling problems with a staff. They have no comment.

"I opened Summerford Design in 1978 in Dallas after eight years with Stan Richards. I put together my portfolio, but I really didn't think I would have to use it much because of my experience with the Richards Group. I was wrong. It was then I discovered that every time you go after business, you have to reintroduce yourself.

"Today, I record all the work I keep on 35mm. I wish there was a better way, but I have yet to find it. I use this as a basic format because of its flexibility. I use the slides for client presentations, show entries, archival purposes, and for presentations at design or art directors' clubs. From time to time, I do have work shot in a 4"x5" format, but only for a special purpose. I don't normally use this larger format when I make an actual portfolio presentation.

"I average a couple of presentations per month. The work I show depends on what the client wants to see. Since I'm the one who sets up the meeting, I usually have a pretty good idea of what the client wants. So, I try to show them a little more than they expected, a few surprises.

"Depending on the number of people present at the meeting, I will use a tray of slides or, if it's a one-on-one meeting, I may just take a sleeve of slides and a stack of printed samples and a copy of my book, *Twenty Years of Summerford Design*. If

Jack Summerford

the client wants to see work I've done in corporate identity, I use a slide presentation because you can't show all the applications well in any other format.

"I like to use actual samples as often as possible, and sometimes will leave a copy of an annual report or corporate capabilities brochure as a leave-behind. I like for the prospective client to have time to really look through the book and see what I've done—how I've handled the organization, the graphics, the type. How the book feels in your hand. I think all of those things are important, and you can't show them in a photograph.

"At the end of a presentation, I may ask the prospective client if he or she would like to keep any of my samples as reference material. I give them the opportunity to pick and choose exactly what they want to keep. I like them to have examples of my work for any in-house meetings that I wouldn't attend. Their choices also give me a good idea of exactly the work they like, and I use that as a starting point when we get down to the specifics."

Ungerman Hill took on a rather unconventional identity for a law firm. Shown are paper applications and drink coasters. I lead off with several strong corporate identity pieces.

Exploration is a fictitious science museum invented for a Simpson Paper Company letterhead paper promotion.

Brochures and a hard hat are part of an identity for Bateson, a general contracting company. This shows both one of a common and an unusual application of a corporate identity program.

This poster was given away at a design conference in Sacramento to anyone who did not get work accepted in a very well-known design show. The conference theme was "Awards and Rewards." I've included it here because it's a well-known piece for the AIGA and a fairly recent work.

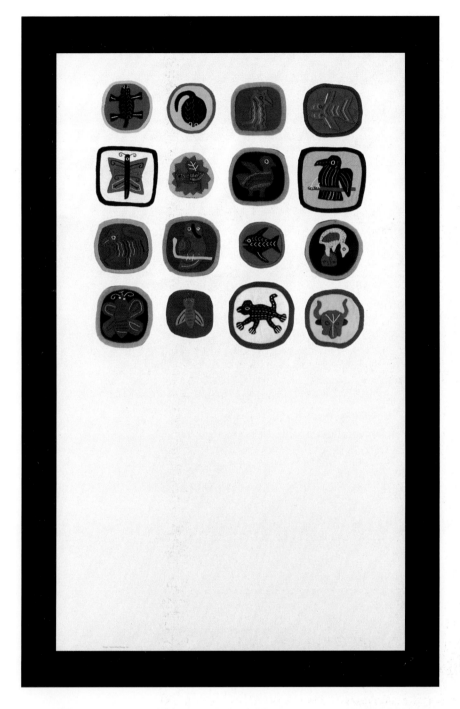

HKS, Inc., a large architectural firm, has a large corporate brochure.

Mola patches seemed appropriate illustrations for Brodnax Printing Company's poster introducing their process color guides.

An illustration from AT&T Teaching Verses, a collection of poems by Diane Cory used in human resource seminars.

and coffee throughout the night. By Sunday, all the lights were back on.

For the 1.5 million customers served by Central and South West's four electric operating companies, it takes the dedication of 8,500 employees to provide reliable service. Behind these employees stands a $9 billion investment in power plants, transmission lines and distribution networks.

When Mother Nature turns out the lights, customers depend on the electric company to turn them back on quickly and safely. Americans have come to have great confidence that this high level of reliability will be available at the flip of a switch.

An Obligation to Serve

The obligation to serve always has been a hallmark of the electric utility industry. Over its 100-year history, the industry has formalized operating guidelines, adopted mutual assistance agreements and built interconnections to exchange power for economy as well as for emergencies. Mother Nature's effect on reliable service, therefore, tends to be on[e] lived. The real threat today to [elec]tric service comes from those [who would] "decontrol" the present syste[m. They pro]pose to deregulate electric [service and] open the electric system to [competition. In] doing, the carefully deve[loped coordination] and control that now e[xists would be re]placed with uncertain[ty] and unproven suppli[ers]. To encourage comp[eti]tion, for example...

incentives for cogenera[tion] produce electricity [as a by-product] for other purposes. [Some] have proposed inc[reased] unregulated co[mpetition from] power produce[rs and] cogenerators, [these pro]ducers have [an incentive to] move in [...] ut wh[...] custo[...] in [...] the[...] s[...]

Twenty Years of Summerford Design is a self-promotion book covering, you guessed it, twenty years of design by Jack Summerford. I include this as a tie-in to my bringing the actual book along. The book's great for showing examples of work in response to specific questions.

This shopping bag is just a small part of a complete identity for Something's Afoot, a sock and hosiery boutique. It brings the presentation full circle—back to corporate identity. It's also a lively, fun piece that helps set a more informal tone for the discussion that follows.

Trademark logo for Jeff Smith, a designer of architectural stained glass.

This annual report for Central and South West Corporation, an electric utility holding company, was both a design and illustration opportunity.

COMMUNICATION ARTS, INC.

"Communication Arts, Inc., has spent the last eighteen years quietly building an international environmental and graphic design practice. Our staff of forty-seven consists of graphic designers, architects, industrial, and interior designers, as well as administrative, project management, and research personnel.

"The work we do is diverse. We design a wide range of architectural, environmental, and printed graphic communications. This includes, for example, redevelopments, retail complexes, restaurants, food courts, fixtures, furnishings, stores, streetscapes, signage programs, sports arenas, public places, recreational resorts, marketing collateral, brochures, identity programs, packaging, and interpretive exhibit programs.

"We tailor our presentations to focus our experience in the area of the client's interest, suggest further capability on our part, and avoid confusion or dismissal for being too general.

"We rely on a variety of portfolio forms to accommodate these issues: the general capabilities brochure, an oversized, wire-bound, four-color, forty-six-page piece that we add to every four to five years; a general slide show, a two-projector, general capabilities review of our best and most recent work, much of which is not in the brochure; a selected slide show, in which we put together a carousel or two of related work that addresses the type of project we are attempting to obtain; and a portfolio of printed samples and/or drawings, which is usually for graphic brochures, identity, and signage systems. Here, we review actual finished pieces with the client.

"Our portfolio is simply a tool that enables us to talk about the client and about ourselves. We present the work in terms of the benefits clients have derived and probably will derive from hiring us. This lets the client know we are on their side, and not promoting a hidden agenda that they have to watch out for. Acknowledging the client and their objectives allows us to build trust and comfort.

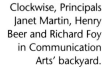

"We also try to learn during our interview who our client is to be. What are their approval processes, personalities, values, schedules, and budgets? What is their team organization and political environment? We ask ourselves if the fit is right and if we will be able to do our best work with this client's team. We try to choose our clients as carefully as they choose us.

Clockwise, Principals Janet Martin, Henry Beer and Richard Foy in Communication Arts' backyard.

"There is also a human dimension to presenting portfolios. We give our best presentations when something unexpected happens or is discussed. The ice is broken when we get past the immediate concerns and really connect on a human level. Common interests, humor, a personal feeling, some insight, or a relevant anecdote are where we look for this opportunity.

"If our work is on a par with or better than others, the punctuation of a spontaneous human interaction enables us at least to be more memorable and, at best, to outpace the others."

Our printed portfolio highlighting marketing and capabilities brochures and major identity programs.

Regional references in architectural details.

"Rhumba" custom light fixture.

Entry, trellises, imagery, signs, furnishings, finishes, fixtures and ornaments are orchestrated to communicate the experience of San Antonio's Rivercenter.

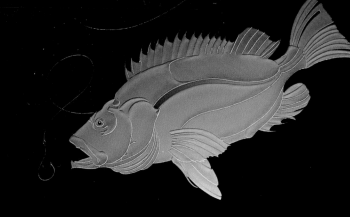

Chicago's Ford City is
transformed into an exciting,
contemporary retail environment.

Respecting regional symbols

acknowledges local lifestyles. This helps build

customer allegiance, creates a unique design,

and gives a competitive edge to our client.

Cruciform-based
identity for Boulder
Community Hospital.

ST. LOUIS UNIO

DINNER IN TH

Car culture—diner–inspired
restaurant design.

"*Everybody seems to love it... The public in St. Louis, and indeed in the middle of the country, has taken the Station to heart.*"

St. Louis Post Dispatch

Riverwalk, New Orleans, graphic and environmental design nods to a marine heritage.

St. Louis Union Station retail planning and amenities interior design for The Rouse Company.

Interpretive directories provide information and build character.

New Jersey's Bridgewater Commons'
center court and signing (below) celebrate
a rural, sophisticated self-image.

Design creates the opportunity for ideas
to be communicated. People intuitively
understand the appropriateness of a
successfully presented environment or idea.

Entry sign design announces
Bayside Marketplace in Miami
for The Rouse Company.

Identity glyph for Hill Partners,
North Carolina.

METROPOLIS
TIMESQUARE

Leasing brochure captures the excitement of Metropolis Times Square, New York, for The Hahn Company.

MAN ITALIA
NEW YORK

Wrought iron and slate signs, painted canvas menus set the tone of the Cordillera Spa, Colorado.

McRay Magleby

"My life has been segmented between the teaching part, the freelance part, and my regular job at Brigham Young University. They overlap a lot because the work I have done at BYU has really gotten me the freelance work. The name on the door says Brigham Young University Graphics, and I am the director of the department. I've been here about twenty years, since I got out of school. We maintain a staff of about ten people—some are student interns, some are part-time students, and some are full-time professional graphic artists. We work on outside projects as well as school projects. We are in the same building as the University Press, so under one roof we can design, write, illustrate, print, and mail out anything we do.

"I was trained as an illustrator, but I prefer to do my own design, incorporating my illustration. When I began working I found that I enjoyed design more than illustration, so I have always worked back and forth between the two. If I work for an art director or a designer, doing just an illustration, I usually won't accept the job unless I have some freedom with the final work.

"I put together my first portfolio when I was ten years old and I decided I wanted to become a Walt Disney animator. I got a paper route to make some money, bought the acetate for cels, did an animation piece and had it shot, and that was my first portfolio. When I was in high school, I made up a pin-striping portfolio with numbered designs. During school my 'clients' would pick out the design they wanted by the page number, and after school I would paint the design on the car. I also had a sign painting portfolio. I always knew that I could earn a living with my talent.

"I'm directing as much work as possible toward designing limited-edition, silk-screened posters—a new area for me. All the work that you see now in my portfolio is silk-screened. We're working to make these multiple-use artworks, and I like working out a piece that is adaptable to many uses.

"I don't think I have a single illustration style, and I guess that's one of the reasons I never relied on just illustration to support me. For example, the illustration of the musical instruments in this portfolio was much more involved and time-consuming than the fruit series, but I am a bluegrass music fanatic and could never do an interpretive work of a Gibson Mastertone banjo. I had to get as close as I possibly could, even though it is silk-screened.

McRay Magleby

"Almost all of the work I do is outside Utah, and people know about me because of the awards I have won and the pieces that appear in a variety of design annuals. I have never entered an illustration competition because I don't normally seek just illustration work. I always keep portfolio material in a form that is handy to be sent out. I have a printed piece that I usually send to people who aren't too familiar with my work and aren't specific about an assignment. When someone has a job, we talk about what they want, and I can put together either slides, 4"x5"s, or printed samples, depending on what they need for their presentation. Many times a designer will need to present my work to a client. I try to make it easy for them.

"I opened with the wave poster because it won the 'Most Memorable Poster in the World' competition and it is probably the most recognizable piece I've ever done. I designed the poster originally to commemorate the fortieth anniversary (1985) of the bombing of Hiroshima. Everything else is registration posters done for Brigham Young University, and the order that I have used them is based on how they look on a spread. I consider a portfolio another design assignment, and I put together my book just as I would a job for a client."

I opened with the wave poster because it won the "Most Memorable Poster in the World" competition
and it is probably the most recognizable piece I've ever done.

Registration posters for Brigham Young University. Because I want to direct as much work as possible into designing limited-edition silk-screeened posters, everything in my portfolio now is silk-screened.

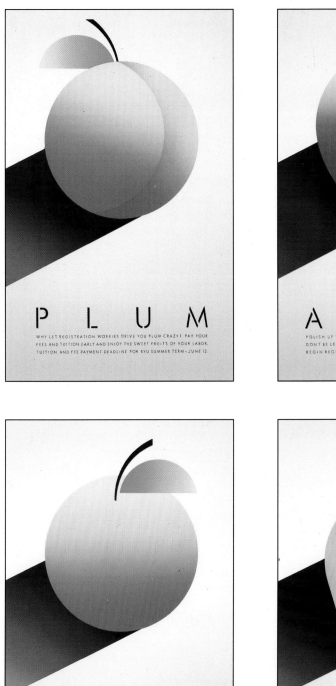

PLUM

WHY LET REGISTRATION WORRIES DRIVE YOU PLUM CRAZY? PAY YOUR
FEES AND TUITION EARLY AND ENJOY THE SWEET FRUITS OF YOUR LABOR.
TUITION AND FEE PAYMENT DEADLINE FOR BYU SUMMER TERM—JUNE 12

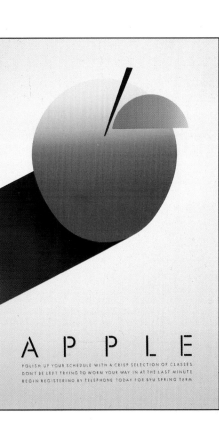

APPLE

POLISH UP YOUR SCHEDULE WITH A CRISP SELECTION OF CLASSES.
DON'T BE LEFT TRYING TO WORM YOUR WAY IN AT THE LAST MINUTE.
BEGIN REGISTERING BY TELEPHONE TODAY FOR BYU SPRING TERM.

ORANGE

PEEL BACK YOUR CLASS SCHEDULE COVER AND ARRANGE A SUCCULENT
SUMMER TERM. DON'T LET POOR SCHEDULING DRAIN YOUR JUICES.
BEGIN REGISTERING BY TELEPHONE TODAY FOR BYU SUMMER TERM.

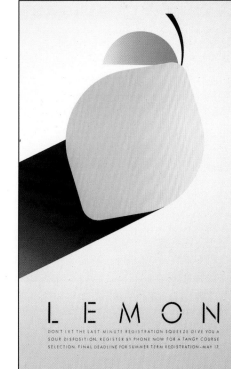

LEMON

DON'T LET THE LAST-MINUTE REGISTRATION SQUEEZE GIVE YOU A
SOUR DISPOSITION. REGISTER BY PHONE NOW FOR A TANGY COURSE
SELECTION. FINAL DEADLINE FOR SUMMER TERM REGISTRATION—MAY 17.

Registration posters for Brigham Young University. All the posters in this portfolio are arranged on the page to
create the most attractive possible spreads.

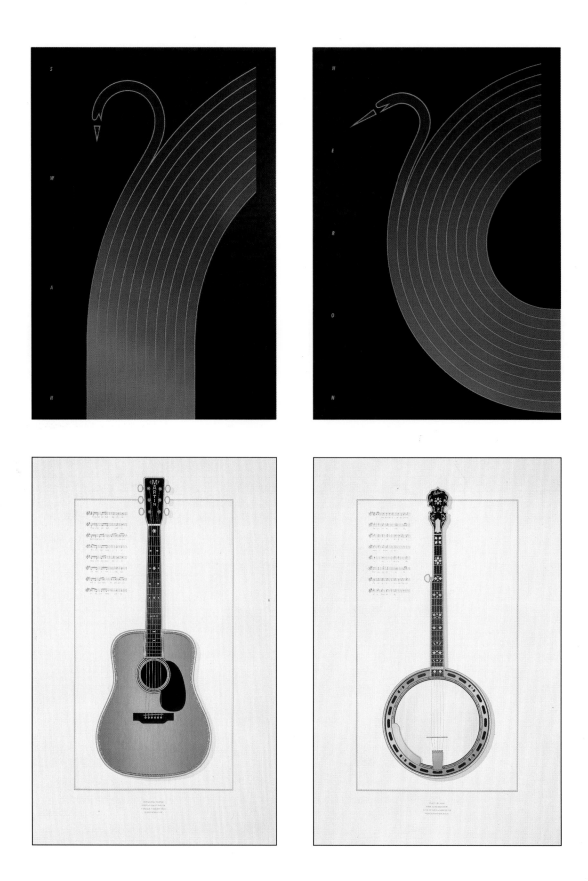

Registration posters for Brigham Young University.

THE ULTIMATE PORTFOLIO

Registration posters for Brigham Young University.

HEATHER COOPER
COMMUNICATION BY DESIGN

"People remember me for different reasons: some for my paintings, some for my illustration, others for my design work. I formed Heather Cooper Communication by Design in Toronto in 1984 to house the common bond running through all aspects of my work. We're a close-knit group, and I like to work in that atmosphere.

"We keep a staff of about six people, and that is a comfortable size for us. We've made a conscious effort to keep this firm small because it allows us to offer our clients more personal service and it allows me constant involvement from the initial conceptual phases through the final stages of each project the firm creates.

"We try to pick our clients as carefully as they pick us and generally make between four and eight presentations per month. At the end of each project, we decide what is to be included in our portfolio, and the work is photographed on a timely basis. This keeps our portfolio material current and relieves us of the responsibility of storing outsized and dimensional samples.

"Since we do work in all areas of graphic design, we don't have just one portfolio to show prospective clients. We tailor each presentation to the particular areas of interest for that client.

"Our presentations are shown as projected 35mm slides for groups of three or more persons, or as mounted, 4"x5" color transparencies with a portable light box for smaller meetings. We show a minimum of eighty transparencies per presentation, mounted four per board.

"When we put together a presentation, I want to open and close with truly successful projects that will catch the client's attention. I don't like a slow start or a slow finish. We will style our portfolio according to the work we're going after, like the packaging presentation shown in this book. In packaging, there is frequently graphic identity to be considered. So we will incorporate logos with the packaging work.

"The identity aspect is really important for package design. Often packaging clients see them as separate things when in fact they're not. It would be crazy to go after packaging projects without showing identities. The identities you show would be applicable to the specific package. For instance, you might show a retail as opposed to a corporate identity to a cosmetics package client.

Heather Cooper

"The only exceptions to transparencies in our portfolio will be the smaller printed samples, such as brochures and reports, which are mainly collateral material, and often a copy of my book, *Carnaval Perpetuel,* which shows a general range of our work. Because the book is also a showcase for my illustration, we may try to incorporate photography in some aspect of the presentation if we think it's necessary. I don't show a separate illustration portfolio because I don't want just illustration assignments. My paintings are often incorporated into our clients' work, but we use whatever art form or style that is appropriate to communicate and motivate. We believe design is not a superficial application of graphic components. Rather, it is a well-planned and integral part of the positioning and marketing of a project. We think of our portfolio organization and presentation in the same way. In the following presentation, we are responsible for all the packaging and graphic identity on all the products except Kimberly-Clark."

In this portfolio presentation, we open with Roots. This captures their attention immediately because it is a very well-known program. Another reason for its inclusion is its general market appeal to men, women and children. We have to work not to get slotted into the food or cosmetics category.

ROOTS
NORTHERN·LAKES

In style, this packaging for Stone County Specialties is not a drastic step from Roots. Even though we've gone from shoes and leather goods to food, the design of the package and label is straghtforward with very little illustration.

I think now we need some color—something different, a change of pace. In this series we show the logo, the labels and packages on the bottles, and close-ups of the art so the client can see the detail and understand the feeling the label conveys. Even if this had been photography rather than my illustration, I would have done the same thing. It's the only way to show detail when you're working with transparencies of printed products mounted on jars.

The Perfect Taste is the final food product in this presentation, and I like keeping the three together. Since the art here is less important to the label than on the Scarborough & Co. product, we photographed the entire label flat to show the detail of this project, going from general to specific.

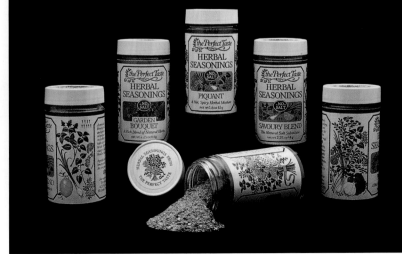

We move on to the redesign of the Yardley graphic identity, showing examples of packaging for a wide variety of products within the assignment, and the development of logos for both existing and new fragrances. I like the idea of contrasting the art of the wooden boxes with the lushness of the rose package.

We will close with Kimberly-Clark Kleenex 100s boxes. Everyone knows about Kleenex, and when you are pitching, everyone has bought the product at some point in their lives and they relate to that. Although this is another general market-base product, decorative packaging is a slightly different assignment than other examples we've shown here. I particularly like to show this lace box because it is a design that printers cannot destroy. That's a very important aspect of the packaging business and a selling point to present to a prospective client.

HUNGRY DOG STUDIO

"'Oh my God, it's those Dixie Dogs from Hell!' is a reaction we've grown accustomed to over the years. In fact, it's become our theme because it usually means a job is not far behind. Hungry Dog Studio is now in its sixth year of business. The studio was formed in August of 1984 and is currently located in Atlanta, Georgia. The studio consists wholly of ourselves, Bob and Val Tillery.

"Since a large percentage of our work is now music industry related, for this book we were asked to present a portfolio that was targeted to this field.

"For this presentation we are showing our work mixed together, but because we are a two-person studio, our portfolio is usually broken down into three sections: Val's work, collaboration work and my work. The collaboration section is the smallest of the three, since this is a new area for us. Sometimes we open with Val's work and sometimes with my work, but we work as a team. We offer our clients two minds instead of one and they seem to respond favorably. We have a similar sense of humor and we collaborate on some concepts even when one of us does the final execution. We tell our clients to decide which one of us they want to do the job. Since this collaboration is a unique aspect to our studio, we feel we should emphasize it.

"Once again, the work in our book is interchangeable to comply with the needs of the individual client, but finally, getting the job is based on calculated luck and being right for a particular sound or feeling.

"Whether we're calling on the client in person or just sending out a sample package, we try to include as much related material as possible. Also included, if the art director or designer hasn't received them already, are our self-promotion projects. Since we feel our work is adaptable to vari-

ous styles of music, we don't limit ourselves by going after only rock 'n' roll clients. And this is where our self-promotion pieces come into play. Through these personal projects, we are able to show the client the different directions we're capable of or that we'd like to venture into, even though we haven't had assignments in these areas yet.

"Since a high percentage of our clients are out of state, making a personal visit is not always possible. When we can't make such visits, we use the 4"x5" transparency format for the presentation. These are mounted on fifteen to twenty 8½"x11" black mats and we number each mat in the upper left hand corner to keep the order straight.

"We enclose a sheet of captions for each numbered piece. We also enclose a set of leave-behind printed samples that can be retained for their files. We rely on overnight express services and the mail to send either our tearsheet samples or our 4"x5" portfolio.

"We try to update our mailouts when new or related samples come in. Self-promotion pieces are updated every six months, once a year maximum.

"It is important to understand that the clients we choose to go after are the result of a great deal of research. We try to find out what kind of stable each record company has and whether we feel we are right for that market. We're very select about who we want to work with. We do this through our sources in the business, like annuals, trade publications, through word-of-mouth and by living in the record stores in our free time."

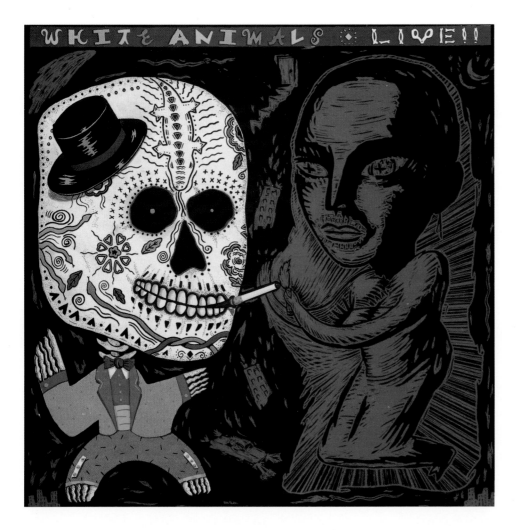

Bob + Val Tillery
Dreadbeat Records, Nashville.
Album cover for *White Animals LIVE!!* We've opened with a strong piece with good recognition in the record industry.

Val Tillery
SBK Records, New York.
Commissioned but unpublished cover for Technotronic's *Pump Up The Jam.*

Val Tillery
Warner Bros. Records, Nashville.
Commissioned but unpublished generic 7" record sleeve.

Val Tillery
Profile Records, New York.
Album cover for *Best of House Music.*

Val Tillery
Profile Records, New York.
Album cover for *Best of House Music Volume 2 Gotta Have House.*

Bob Tillery
Reprise/Warner Bros. Records, Los Angeles. 12" single cover for *Dog In The Road (Of Life)*/Marc Anthony Thompson. © 1989 Reprise Records for the U.S. and WEA International, Inc. for the world outside of the U.S. Used by kind permission of Reprise Records.

Bob Tillery
Profile Records, New York. 12"
single cover for *Papa Crazy*/
Run-D.M.C.

Bob Tillery
Reprise/Warner Bros. Records,
Nashville. Album cover for *I Am
Just A Rebel*/Billy Hill.

Val Tillery
Polygram Records, New York.
Commissioned but unpublished
cover for *Stairway To Heaven*/
Highway To Hell compilation.

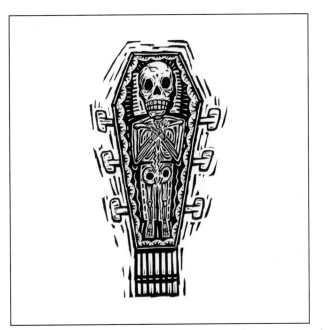

STAIRWAY TO HEAVEN / HIGHWAY TO HELL

OZZY OSBOURNE ▪ SCORPIONS ▪ SKID ROW

FEATURING: BON JOVI ▪ JASON BONHAM

CINDERELLA ▪ GORKY PARK ▪ MOTLEY CRÜE

Bob Tillery
Polygram Records, New York.
Cover for *Stairway To Heaven/Highway To Hell* compilation.

Bob + Val Tillery
My Theme Song (This Week) series of self-promo cards. The portfolio includes strong self-promotion pieces that lead into future follow-up mailings.

(Opposite page)
Bob + Val Tillery
Your Heaven Is My Hell collaboration piece from one-man show in Nashville, "Cows, Punks & Propaganda."

Val Tillery
Posters for Marc Anthony Thompson, Los Angeles.
Announcement for club dates.

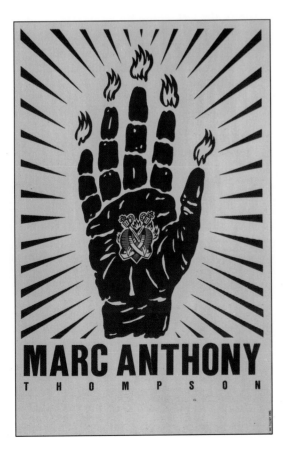

GARY KELLEY

"As a freelance illustrator working in the university town of Cedar Falls, Iowa, my only true portfolios are 1,000 miles east in New York City with my agent, Richard Solomon. He keeps two tasteful, leather-bound books for showing around the city and another pair of similar, but smaller, less expensive 'traveling books' for filling requests from other parts of the country. We organized these portfolios together, and Richard updates them frequently, with my approval. I produce a volume of work, so there's seldom a shortage of material.

"In putting together the portfolios, Richard and I have included a range of areas in which I am most comfortable. We show a lot of human interest, a few portraits, and a little landscape work. We show only my pastel work, but we show it in a couple of stylistic variations. My Cubist-influenced work occupies about one half of the portfolio and my more traditional, impressionistic work occupies the other half. The flow and quality of these new pieces is what dictates the frequency of the updates, and often some very tough decisions have to be made—for example, what can be eliminated to make room for the new entries.

"We show neatly trimmed printed material (tearsheets) mounted on black pages covered with acetate sleeves. Oversized printed material is either replaced with C-print photographs or added loose to the portfolio as laminated pieces. The portfolios themselves are forty pages, one image per page. Presentations are made in response to specific requests from publishers, agencies, corporate art departments, and designers. About 10 percent of my work is pure advertising. The remaining 90 percent is a fairly even mix of book, editorial, and institutional assignments. The buyers have usually seen a small sampling of my work in the Richard Solomon promotional mailers and are asking to see more. About 60 percent of the work now comes through my agent, with the other 40 percent coming in as a result of an established reputation due to continued success in various annuals: *Communication Arts Illustration Annual, American Illustration,* and the Society of Illustrators annual.

Gary Kelley

"Since I do not keep an 'official' portfolio in my Cedar Falls studio, I respond to direct requests to see more work with neatly organized sheets of slides. One advantage in doing this is the ability to tailor the presentation to a client's particular needs. I don't really fill a lot of slide requests, maybe a couple per month. Usually an art director has already decided he wants to use me before the call comes in, so it's more a matter of working out technicalities than it is showing new work. Again, my presence in the various annuals has led to this luxury. These annuals, along with Richard's promotional mailings and ads in the *American Illustration Showcase* directories, are invaluable tools. I could not be successful without them or the portfolios that travel around New York City and the country."

I opened with Power Broker, a *Chicago Times* magazine page, for two reasons. It's not only an award-winning piece but also a personal favorite. I feel it's one of the strongest pieces in my Cubist style because it has the most edge.

Summer Fiction, *North American Review* magazine cover

Café Society, a Cole-Haan shoe catalog cover

Russian Constructivism, J. B. Speed Art Museum poster

G. Keeley

closed with Rugby Match, a limited edition print for Charter Hospitals, and 19th Century Studies, a Drew University poster to provide a strong o
o punch of my more traditional style. Although Rugby Match is an older piece, I keep it in my portfolio because it has brought in a lot of work
me. It just seems to catch the eyes of art directors. 19th Century Studies is a fairly new piece, and one of the best in this more traditional style

MELISSA GRIMES

"After twelve years as a freelance illustrator, my portfolio has evolved a lot—from matted pieces or original artwork when I was just out of school to plastic pages showing a whole arsenal of various illustration 'styles' as a beginning freelancer—and now finally to printed tearsheets that I can select and send to prospective clients according to the nature of the illustration work they need.

"I don't often show an unsolicited portfolio anymore. Generally, a client calls me, having seen my work in a magazine or in one of the national illustration annuals (*American Illustration, Print,* or *Communication Arts*). They already know what my work looks like and are interested in using it, but want to see a few more examples. I send them, usually by overnight delivery. Next morning, those samples may be used to get final approval for a job. That's how an illustration assignment *begins.*

"But it's showing a portfolio when your work is unknown that's the hard part. I remember it well—waiting clammy handed in mirrored reception areas for art directors who were always busy or late; making small talk while someone pored silently over my portfolio; finding a place to park!

"The illustrations on this and the next few pages are some I might show an advertising client. Most of my illustrations that have been seen nationally and in annuals are editorial. Most use bright colors, surreal or bizarre subject matter, and are crowded with objects. Consequently, I'm not thought of as often when advertising or corporate jobs come up, and I don't have many out-and-out advertising pieces in my portfolio. I want to do more advertising and corporate work, if only to show that I can handle simpler, more conservative, or serious subject matter. It's irritating to hear 'Your work is too wild for our client' as often as I do, so I've tried to include pieces that show other facets of my work."

Melissa Grimes

This illustration, from Royal Viking Lines' promotional magazine *Skald*, shows the heroic nature of travel throughout history. It shows the product—the cruise ship—in a surrealistic collage context. Although it was done for a corporate magazine and has the feel of an editorial illustration, it is advertising work.

AS LONG AS IT'S MILD.

MILD 100's

One of my few true advertising illustrations is this Benson & Hedges Mild 100s ad, one of a series done for Ted Bates Advertising in London. The colors in the illustration echo those of the purple, white and gold cigarette pack. The image and color scheme are (for me) unusually calm and subdued, and I like to bring this out when people say my colors are too bright for their project. I think it's also good to show that I've worked with a big international agency.

I made my business cards on a color copying machine.

131

FILM SAN ANTONIO

Most colleges only see one side of you

These days, most colleges act as if students just want all the right formulas, facts and figures. But we at the University of St. Thomas believe students want to develop another side as well. The side that yearns to know more about themselves, their relationship to the world of culture and even possibly the meaning behind it all. If you'd like to know more about our undergraduate or graduate programs for both sides of you, call us at 713/522-7916.

UST
University of
St. Thomas
Houston

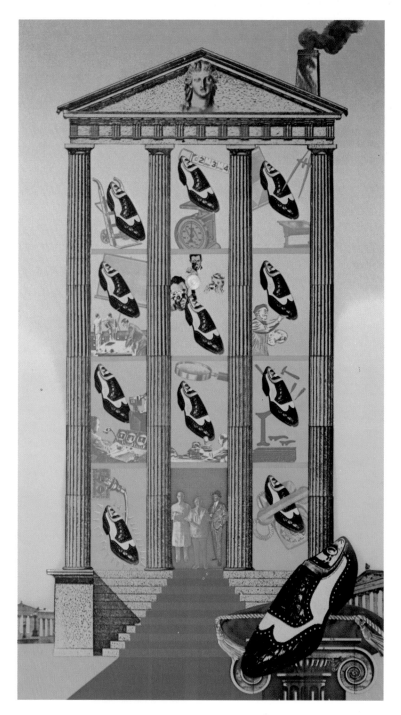

(Top) I include the billboard illustration for the San Antonio Film Commission for several reasons. First, it's my only collage billboard in recent years. Also, it's a good example of my engraving-based collage. And it has a simple, uncluttered composition and subdued color scheme which contrasts well with other pieces in the portfolio. (Right)The temple of shoes is one of a series I did for ByVideo, Inc., who make point-of-purchase video machines. The shoe represents a product being taken through the various stages of research and production of a video. This shows that I can understand and interpret the details of a client's business. It also shows the kind of color I often like to use. The background is airbrushed acrylic paint, and I like to show that I have some (if minimal) airbrush skills. (Above) Black-and-white illustration assignments come up now and then, and I want to show I can do them. This newspaper ad was made with blown-up halftones and engravings, with a reversal of computer-generated letters and symbols as a background.

(Above) The Halloween candy catalog cover for McLane Trucking Company is several years old, but it stays in the portfolio. It combines four-color and one-color illustration work, engraving, and color copies, and shows copies made from three-dimensional objects (the candy). I just did a series of three similar catalog covers for another client, and I know it was this piece that got me the assignment. (Left) Dorsey Press, a publisher of scholarly books, commissioned this cover for all their catalogs, so it contains images representing all categories of books they publish, from social studies to anthropology to political science. It's a good example of using collage to solve complicated illustration problems with a single image.

133

(Above) This is an unpublished illustration for a company called Computerpals which links classrooms around the world via computer networks. The idea was to show international cooperation among young people and the kinds of knowledge they could obtain. The illustration is different from most of my work in that it uses an illustrated border as well as blueprints and high-quality photographic prints instead of photocopies. Since the illustration hasn't yet been printed, I willl show a color print or an 8"x10" transparency of it instead of a tearsheet. (Right) "Get Shrimpnotized" was a menu insert for Bennigan's restaurants. It's a good injection of humor into the portfolio and almost always gets a laugh. I don't have very many pieces of point-of-purchase consumer advertising like this, so it fills that category. It's also an interesting combination of cut paper, engravings and photography.

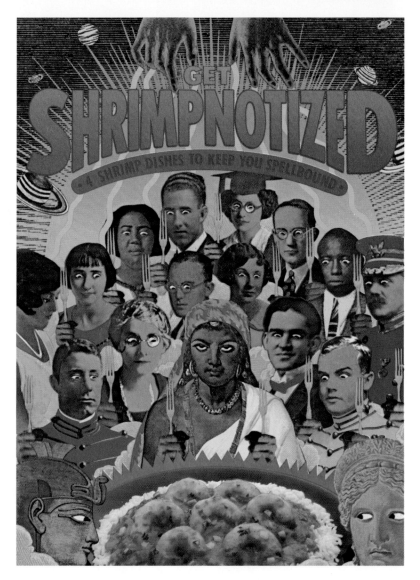

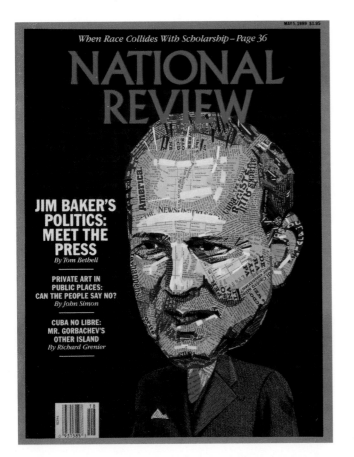

NATIONAL REVIEW

JIM BAKER'S POLITICS: MEET THE PRESS
By Tom Bethell

PRIVATE ART IN PUBLIC PLACES: CAN THE PEOPLE SAY NO?
By John Simon

CUBA NO LIBRE: MR. GORBACHEV'S OTHER ISLAND
By Richard Grenier

CONTINUUM

Volume 7 Number 1 | A Publication of the Continuum Company | Spring, 1989

(Top left) The portrait of James Baker for the cover of *National Review* shows an unusual collage technique that I had never attempted before this assignment. To emphasize his close relations with the press, Baker's face is made up of hundreds of small pieces of newspaper type. I was surprised at the good likeness I was able to get, and I will keep this piece in my portfolio in hopes of getting similar assignments. If they didn't see this, most art directors would probably never think of using collage as a medium for portraiture! (Top right) The image of a globe is one that comes up often, and because of that, it's a challenge to find new ways to use it—in this case with countries made of international currency. The client, Continuum, an insurance software manufacturer, was devoting an entire issue of its corporate publication to its international expansion plans and wanted the globe to be included in some way. The Continuum cover is one of the more conservative pieces in my current portfolio. It also shows a collage style based on old engravings rather than photographs. This style generally looks more "traditional" and less surreal than the photocollages do. (Left) The ad for Southwest Airlines' Airfreight service shows symbols representing items the airline *can't* carry—for instance, the mummy indicated they won't ship bodies. It uses collage almost as spot illustrations, disconnected from one another, and therefore is a good portfolio piece since it presents my work in a new way. It's one of a series of three ads, all made up of these "spot" collages.

JAMES MCMULLAN

"I started doing freelance illustration jobs for small publishers and *Harper's* magazine while I was still at Pratt Institute, but I began to totally support myself through illustration in 1960.

"Until my three-year stint at The Pushpin Studio from 1965 to 1968, I had worked alone. After Pushpin, I saw that I would be more efficient with an assistant. Through the intervening years I have had from one to three people working for me. At the moment, I have two, one of whom works on allied but independent illustration projects and one of whom deals with administrative work, research, and the like.

"My work is all based on my images, although more and more of it, like my Lincoln Center posters, includes my design and lettering. My clients run a fairly wide gamut: large and small magazines, design firms, nonprofit organizations like libraries and hospitals, adult and children's book publishers, large corporations like Mobil, individuals who commission images for personal albums, and cultural institutions like the Lincoln Center Theatre in New York City.

"I haven't sent out an unsolicited portfolio in several years. Most of the time a portfolio is requested by a designer or art director to show a client or an editor, for instance, so that person will feel comfortable with the art director's choice. Occasionally an art director will not know my work, but will see one piece in an annual or a magazine and will want to see more examples. On average, two to three portfolios are requested a week by potential clients. I tailor each presentation, based on the call that comes in.

"My portfolio consists of single-mounted pieces so I am able to tailor it each time to the particular subject matter or mood of the job. Sometimes that means putting an emphasis on realistic editorial pieces or, at the other end of the spectrum, choosing pieces that are more stylized and graphic. Sometimes an art director asks for a 'general portfolio,' and then I include a variety of work.

James McMullan

"I try to make the portfolio, in any case, representative of my best work or at least the kind of work I want to do. This means that jobs that for one reason or another didn't work out as well as they might have don't get mounted as portfolio pieces, no matter how practical they might be for showing the solution to a certain kind of problem. I see the portfolio as a kind of explanation to the world of what I like and what I'm like, as well as showing how I can be useful.

"I don't have a representative and except for a brief period in 1969, have not had one, so my portfolio is usually sent to the client by messenger. I think this is okay for me at this point in my career, but I think it's important for younger illustrators to arrange for as many face-to-face interviews as they can. Often the work will make a great deal more sense to the art director if they get a chance to see and talk to the illustrator."

Anything Goes, 1987
For the Lincoln Center Theatre production of the 1930s Cole Porter musical. The play is set on board an oceanliner and its main character is a revivalist cabaret singer, Reno Sweeny. I put this piece first because it's the most well-known.

The NYC Marathon, 1988
An image for the annual New York City Marathon which was used in magazines, city buses and on street posters. It is meant to suggest a fragment from a Greek vase.

Cats Poster, 1987
This illustrates aspects of cat activitity like leaping, stretching, yawning and watching. This is an insert poster for the kindergarden magazine *Let's Find Out.* The children imitated the actions of the cats on the poster.

Bronx Zoo Poster, 1989
A poster commemorating the opening of the renovated Elephant Building at the Bronx Zoo.

THE ULTIMATE PORTFOLIO

Hampton Library, 1987
The first of a series of three annual posters announcing
an auction for the Bridge Hampton, New York Library.
The overall theme for these posters is reading in the
Hamptons. Located on the Long Island shore, the area
is famous for its beaches and resort living.

Hampton Library, 1988
The second in the series
shows a different aspect of
reading in the Hamptons.

Hampton Library, 1989
This time the subject
of the poster was a
youthful reader.

The Front Page, 1987
This play is a 1930s melodrama taking place in the press room of a prison. This Lincoln Center production involved a group of hardboiled newspaper reporters.

THE HECHT & MacARTHUR'S
FRONT PAGE
LINCOLN CENTER THEATER at the VIVIAN BEAUMONT

Death and the King's Horsemen, 1987
A Lincoln Center Production poster for a very ritualized play about ceremonial suicide in a Nigerian tribe.

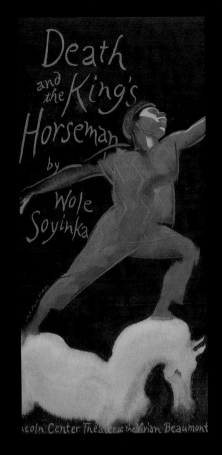

Measure For Measure, 1989
This image suggests the relationship between evil and purity that is one of the central issues of this Shakesperian plot. The poster also hints at the fact that production was done in modern costume. A Lincoln Center Production.

Road, 1988
A contemporary British playwright describing the desperate lives of the poor in East London. It was both bitter and very funny. A Lincoln Center Production.

The Tenth Man, 1989
A poster for the Lincoln Center revival of Paddy Chayevsky's play. The poster deals with the last act paroxysm of an exorcism. This series of posters shows some of my most recent work, ending with an exceptionally powerful piece.

SOURCES OF INFORMATION

MAGAZINES, ANNUALS AND SHOWS

Art Directors Annual of New York; ADLA Annual; American Illustration; Annual of American Illustration; The Book Show (AIGA); CA Magazine, Advertising and Illustration Annuals; Communication Graphics; Creativity (Art Direction Magazine); DESI Awards (Graphic Design:USA); Graphis Magazine and Annual Reports, Packaging, Illustration, Poster Annuals; HOW Magazine; Mead Annual Report Show; The One Show (NY); Print's Casebooks, Best in Advertising, Covers & Posters, Annual Reports, Packaging, Exhibition Design, Environmental Graphics, Print Magazine and Regional Design Annual; Society of Publication Designers Annual; Typography (Type Directors Club); U&lc.

SOURCE BOOKS

Standard Directory of Advertising Agencies
National Register Publishing Company
866 Third Avenue
New York, New York 10022

Selling Your Graphic Design & Illustration
St. Martin's Press
175 Fifth Avenue
New York, New York 10010

Literary Market Place
Magazine Industry Market Place
R. R. Bowker Company
245 West Seventeenth Street
New York, New York 10011

Graphic Artists Guild Handbook
Pricing & Ethical Guidelines

The Graphic Artists Guild Corporate Design Directory
North Light Books
1507 Dana Avenue
Cincinnati, Ohio 45207

Creative Registry (Primarily for job seekers)
233 East Ontario Street
Suite 500
Chicago, Illinois 60611

DIRECTORIES

American Showcase (Corporate, Illustration)
724 Fifth Avenue
New York, New York 10019

The Creative Blackbook
115 Fifth Avenue
New York, New York 10003

Chicago Creative Directory
333 North Michigan Avenue
Suite 810
Chicago, Illinois 60601

The Workbook
940 North Highland Avenue
Suite B
Los Angeles, California 90038

CLUBS OR ASSOCIATIONS

American Institute of Graphic Arts
1059 Third Avenue
New York, New York 10021

Graphic Artists Guild
11 West 20th Street
New York, New York 10011

Society of Illustrators
128 East 63rd Street
New York, New York 10021

Society of Publication Designers
60 East 42nd Street
Suite 1416
New York, New York 10165

American Center for Design
233 East Ontario Street
Suite 500
Chicago, Illinois 60611

Art Directors' Club of Los Angeles
7080 Hollywood Blvd.
Suite 410
Los Angeles, California 90028

American Illustration
67 Irving Place
New York, New York 10003

Art Directors Club of New York
250 Park Avenue South
New York, New York 10003

The One Club
3 West 18th Street
New York, New York 1001

CREDITS

Author's photo by Carl Fischer Photography.

Identity program designs on pp. 9, 13, and 52-53 © Chermayeff & Geismar Associates. Used with permission from Chermayeff & Geismar Associates.

Time Warner, Inc. 1989 Annual Report by Frankfurt Gips Balkind, © 1990 by Time Warner, Inc. Used with permission from Frankfurt Gips Balkind.

Advertisement for Larson, Ball & Gould, Inc. and Carton Design for Blue Bell Creameries, Inc. © Lyle Metzdorf, Inc. Used with permission from Lyle Metzdorf, Inc.

Cover for KPMG Peat Marwick magazine, World © Anthony Russell, Inc. Used with permission from Anthony Russell, Inc.

All illustrations and photographs in promotional piece for Bookstop bookstores on p. 13, self-promotion piece and How to Be Texan on p. 73 © 1990 by Hixo, Inc. Used with permission from Hixo, Inc.

"Sunrise to Sunrise" brochure, collateral for Arthur International Sales & Marketing, ads for Austin Rover Cars of America, and self-promotional pieces © by Joel Fuller, Pinkhaus Design. Used with permission from Joel Fuller, Pinkhaus Design Corp., 2424 South Dixie Highway, Ste. 201, Miami, FL 33133, (305) 854-1000.

Illustrations on pp. 16-17 © John Alcorn. Used with permission from John Alcorn.

Illustrations on pp. 18-19 © John Robinette. Used with permission from John Robinette.

Personal projects, p. 21; Time magazine covers, p. 23; American Family magazine logo, p. 23; Stars & Stripes (text by Delphine Hirasuna, illustration by various designers), p. 27; and Vegetables (text by Delphine Hirasuna), p. 27 © Kit Hinrichs. Calendar for William Sloan YMCA and Chase Manhattan Bank posters and ad, pp. 22-23 © Kit Hinrichs/Anthony Russell. Crystal Geyser Mineral Water ad (illustration: Graphics Group, Atlanta), p 23; McCall's magazine spread (photographer: Dennis Bettercourt, illustrators: Lynne Dennis & Ellen Blonder, designers: Kit Hinrichs & Gillian Smith), p. 23; Hills Brothers Coffee ad (photographers: John Blaustein & Tom Tracy), p 23; and Hinrichs Design Association Promo (art director: Kit Hinrichs, designer: Paul Hardy, illustrators: Skip Andrews, Guy Billout, Christoph Blumrich, John Clarke, Carveth Kramer, Tim Lewis, George Masi, Marvin Mattelson, Frank Mayo, Nancy Stahl, & Phillipe Weisbecker), p. 24 © Hinrichs Design Association. Warner Communications, Inc. Annual Reports, 1976 & 1977 (art director & designer: Kit Hinrichs, photographers: Phil Marco & John Olron), p. 24; The Potlatch Corporation Annual Report, 1983 (photographer: Tom Tracy, illustrators: Justin Carroll, Will Nelson, & Colleen Quinn), p. 25; AIGA poster (designer: Kit Hinrichs, photographer: Terry Heffernan), p. 25; and Oakland Athletics promo (art director: Richard Silverstein of Ogilvy & Mather, designer: Kit Hinrichs, illustrator: David McMacken), p. 25 © Jonson Pedersen Hinrichs & Shakery. MGM/UA Communications Co. Annual Report, 1986 (art director: Kit Hinrichs, designers: Kit Hinrichs & Karen Berndt, photographers: Terry Heffernan, Barry Robinson, Eric Myer, illustrators: Doug Johnson & Dave Stevenson), p. 25; Immunex Annual report, 1988 (art director: Kit Hinrichs, designers: Kit Hinrichs & Belle How, photographer: Steve Firebaugh, illustrators: Jack Unruh, Wilson McLean, Ed Lindlof, Douglas Fraser, John Craig, & Dave Stevenson), p. 26; Skald magazine cover & spread (art director: Kit Hinrichs, designers: Kit Hinrichs & Sandra McHenry, photographer: Henrik Kam, iIustrators: Melissa Grimes, Jack Unruh, et al.), p. 26; The Many Faces of Mao, Pentagram Papers, #17 (art director: Linda Hinrichs, designer Natalie Kitamura, photographer: Barry Robinson), p. 73; American President Companies 1989 Calendar (art director: Kit Hinrichs, designers: Kit Hinrichs & Sandra McHenry, photographer: Terry Heffernan), p. 27; and identity and packaging for The Nature Company (catalog—art director: Kit Hinrichs, designer: Natalie Kitamura, photographer: Barry Robinson; calendar cube—art director: Kit Hinrichs, designer: Karen Boone, photographer: Gary Oberacre) pp. 13 & 27 © Pentagram San Francisco.

Illustrations on pp. 31-37 © Douglas Fraser. Used with permission from Douglas Fraser.

Pieces on pp. 39-45 © by Claudia De Castro. Used with permission from Claudia De Castro.

Illustrations on pp. 46-47 © Dave Jonason.

Used with permission from Dave Jonason.

Illustrations on pp. 48-49 and self-promotion booklet on p. 75 © Jack Unruh. Used with permission from Jack Unruh.

Designs for identity and packaging programs on pp. 50-51 and general construction brochure for M. A. Segale, Inc. on p. 12 © Hornall Anderson Design Works. Used with permission from Hornall Anderson Design Works.

Photo of Louise Fili on p. 60 by William Duke.

Illustration for cover of Hoopla and "Cowboy on Vacation" © Susi Kilgore. Used with permission from Susi Kilgore.

Brewer-Cantelmo cases, portfolio, and other products on pp. 66, 68, and 70 provided courtesy of Brewer-Cantelmo, 116 East 27th St., New York, New York 10016, (212) 685-1200. All products are custom made; information available on request from Brewer-Cantelmo. Photos by Alpha Commercial Studio, Inc., Ted Pawlyshyn.

Items from Sam Flax's line of presentation materials on pp. 67-69 and 71 provided courtesy of Sam Flax. Sam Flax store locations include 12 W. 20th St., New York, New York 10011, (212) 620-3038 and five other New York City locations; 1460 Northside Dr., Atlanta, GA 30318, (404) 352-7200 and (800) 233-3736; 3407 Bay to Bay Blvd., Tampa FL, (813) 831-3911 and (800) 221-3529; and 1401 E. Colonial Dr., Orlando, FL 32803 (407) 898-9785 and (800) 330-3529. Photos by Alpha Commercial Studio, Inc., Ted Pawlyshyn.

"Cocolat," Morla Design Christmas gift, 1988, © Morla Design, Inc. Used with permission from Morla Design, Inc.

Self-promotion folder p. 74 © 1989 by Tom Curry. Used with permission from Tom Curry.

Self-promotion piece p. 74 by John Field. Used with permission from John Field.

"Seed" self-promotion piece p. 75 © by Norman Green and Jerry Anton. Used with permission from Norman Green and Jerry Anton.

Pieces on pp. 82-83 © by Annie Huang. Used with permission from Annie Huang.

Illustrations on pp. 85-87 © by Marc Burckhardt. Used with permission from Marc Burckhardt.

Pieces on pp. 88-93 © by Runyan/Hinsche Associates. Used with permission from Runyan/HInsche Associates.

Photograph of Jack Summerford on p. 94 by Gary McCoy.

Pieces on pp. 95-99 © by Jack Summerford. Used with permission from Jack Summerford.

Photo of Communication Arts' principals on p. 100 by Steve Collector, courtesy of Communication Arts Incorporated. On p. 101, Communication Arts' brochure—photo by Bill Farrell/The Photo Works, courtesy of Communication Arts Incorporated; and Rivercenter—Owner/Developer: Williams Realty/ Edward J. DeBartolo Company, Project Architect: Urban Design Group, Project Designer: Communication Arts Incorporated, Photos by R. Greg Hursley. Courtesy of Communication Arts Incorporated. On p. 102, Ford City—Owner /Developer: Equity Properties & Development Co., Project Architect: Loebl Schlossman Hackl, Inc., Project Designer: Communication Arts Incorporated, Photo by R. Greg Hursley. Courtesy of Communication Arts Incorporated; Boulder Community Hospital logo—Client: Boulder Community Hospital, Graphic Designer: Communication Arts Incorporated; The Oasis Diner (now called the L.A. Diner)—Owners: Alan & Tania Schwartz, Project Designer: Communication Arts, Incorporated. Photo by Geoffrey Wheeler. Courtesy of Communication Arts Incorporated. On p. 103, St. Louis Union Station—Owner/Developer: Oppenheimer Properties, Inc., Project Architect: Hellmuth, Obata & Kassabaum, Inc., Project Designer: Communication Arts Incorporated. Photo by Wm. E. Mathis. Courtesy of Communication Arts Incorporated; Louisiana World's Fair—Project Architect: Perez Associates Architects, Project Designer: Communication Arts Incorporated. Photo by Andrew Kramer. Courtesy of Communication Arts Incorporated; Riverwalk, a project of The Rouse Company—Architect: Perez Associates Architects, Project Designer: Communication Arts Incorporated; Photo by Timothy Hursley. Courtesy of

Communication Arts Incorporated. On p. 104, Bridgewater Commons—Owner/Developer: The Hahn Company, Project Architect: Anthony Belluschi Architects, Ltd, Project Designer: Communication Arts Incorporated. Photo by R. Greg Hursley, Inc.. Courtesy of Communication Arts Incorporated; Bayside Marketplace—a project of The Rouse Company, Architect: Benjamin Thompson Associates, Project Designer: Communication Arts Incorporated, Photos by R. Greg Hursley, Inc. Courtesy of Communication Arts Incorporated; Hill Partners Logo—Client: Hill Partners, Graphic Designer: Communication Arts Incorporated. On p. 105, Metropolis Times Square brochure—Client: The Hahn Company, Graphic Designer: Communication Arts Incorporated; Cordillera Signage & Logo—Client: Kensington Land Investment partners, Graphic Designer: Communication Arts Incorporated, Photo by R. Greg Hursley. Courtesy of Communication Arts Incorporated; Cordillera's Restaurant Picasso Menu—Client: Kensington Land Investment Partners, Graphic Designer: Communication Arts Incorporated; Amador logo—Client: Centennial Partners Limited, Graphic Designer: Communication Arts Incorporated; 4-UR Ranch logo—Client: Leavell Properties, Graphic Designer: Communications Arts Incorporated; Manitalia logo—Client: Alex Major and Noah Keusch, Graphic Designer: Communication Arts Incorporated.

Posters on pp. 106-111 © McRay Magleby, Provo, Utah. Used with permission from McRay Magleby.

Designs for identity and packaging on pp. 112-117 © Heather Cooper, Communication by Design, Toronto, Canada. Used with permission from Heather Cooper, Communication by Design.

Photo of Bob and Val Tillery, p. 118 by Empire Studio. Album cover for Best of House Music illustration by Val Tillery/Hungry Dog Studio, album cover © 1988 by Profile Records, Inc. Album cover illustration for Best of House Music Volume 2 Gotta Have House by Val Tillery/Hungry Dog Studio, © 1988 by Profile Records, Inc. Twelve inch single cover illustration for Dog In The Road (Of Life) by Bob Tillery/Hungry Dog Studio, © 1989 Reprise Records for the U.S. and WEA International Inc. for the world outside of the U.S.; used by kind permission of Reprise Records. Twelve inch single cover illustration for Papa Crazy/Run-D.M.C. by Bob Tillery/Hungry Dog Studio, © 1989 Profile Records, Inc. Album cover illustration for I Am Just a Rebel/Billy Hill by Bob Tillery/Hungry Dog Studio, © 1989 Reprise Records for the U.S. and WEA International Inc. for the world outside of the U.S.; used by kind permission of Reprise Records. Album cover © 1989 Polygram Records, Inc., illustration by Bob Tillery/Hungry Dog Studio; used by permission from Polygram, from the album Stairway to Heaven/Highway to Hell. Commissioned but unpublished illustration (b/w linoleum block print of skeleton/guitar) for album cover for Stairway to Heaven/Highway to Hell by Val Tillery/Hungry Dog, album cover © 1989 Polygram Records, Inc.; used by permission by Polygram, from the album Stairway to Heaven/Highway to Hell. Your Heaven is My Hell © 1988 Bob + Val Tillery. My Theme Song (This Week)—"Run Through the Jungle" & "Fire" © 1989 by Bob Tillery and "Walking After Midnight" © 1989 by Val Tillery. Album cover illustration for White Animals LIVE!! © 1986 by Bob + Val Tillery. Unpublished cover illustration for Pump Up the Jam, Marc Anthony Russell posters, and generic 7" record sleeve © 1989 by Val Tillery.

All illustrations on pp. 125-129 © by Cary Kelley. Used with permission from Gary Kelley.

Photo on p. 130 by Richard Whittington. All illustrations on pp. 130-135 © Melissa Grimes. Used with permission from Melissa Grimes.

Illustrations on pp. 137-141 © by James McMullan.

INDEX